LIFE IN A DAY

Doris Grumbach

LIFE IN A DAY

BEACON PRESS
BOSTON

Beacon Press
25 Beacon Street
Boston, Massachusetts 02108-2892

Beacon Press books
are published under the auspices of
the Unitarian Universalist Association of Congregations.

01   00   99   98   97   96   8   7   6   5   4   3   2   1

Nude Descending a Staircase, No. 2 by Marcel Duchamp, reprinted by permission
from the Philadelphia Museum of Art: The Louise and Walter Arensberg Collection

The Cry by Edvard Munch, William Francis Warden Fund, courtesy Museum of
Fine Arts, Boston

Photograph of Bolton Abbey © copyright Walter Scott (Bradford) Ltd.

LIBRARY OF CONGRESS CATALOGING-IN-PUBLICATION DATA

Grumbach, Doris.
        Life in a day / Doris Grumbach.
        p. cm.
        Includes bibliographical references.
        ISBN 0-8070-7088-2 (cloth)
        1. Grumbach, Doris—Biography.   2. Women novelists, American—20th
century—Biography.   3. Maine—Social life and customs.   I. Title.
PS3557.R83Z47   1996
813'.54—dc20
[B]   96-13837

For the Sybil ... who speaks truth unadorned.

LIFE IN A DAY

THERE HAVE BEEN A FEW IMPORTANT DAYS recently in my life: in one I heard the news from a friend who was told she had a mortal illness and would die very soon. Some months ago there was a day of high drama: the one-hundred-year-old house down the road burned to the ground, consuming the possessions of generations of Maine-loving summer people. And there was the catastrophic day on which one of my acquaintances, eight miles away, died of AIDS. I have ruled against all of these as subjects for a journal because I have decided to explore twenty-four hours of ordinariness. The common day is more representative of the contents of most of our lives; disastrous ones are rare.

This day holds only one chance of drama. The mail may bring me an early clipping from the *New York Times Sunday Book Review* about my new novel. Otherwise it promises to have very little memorable about it. But I want to write about it because it is precisely like most of the more than twenty-five hundred days I have lived through on Billings Cove. Only specificity, the details, differ. Still, without special distinction, it is a day in which I find myself unusually aware, at almost every moment, of what is happening in my house, my village, my head. It is one during which there is continuing deterioration in Washington, the city I had left behind, and storms and stresses in the country at large. But my usual distress at political events does not affect me this day. The uneventful calm of the village I have adopted blinds and deafens me to the absurd, unending trial of a famous sports hero for two horrifying murders. In this place I have myself committed a minor act of violence against nature by catching a destructive chipmunk in a Havaheart trap.

In most lives, as in mine, such hypersensitive days are rare. It is as though, for once, our entire selves have been turned inside out, so that subcutaneous layers of awareness are suddenly exposed to the light and heat. If I sit in a quiet room, I do not hear the distant sounds of the furnace, or the refrigerator, or the invasive chipmunks (could it be mice?) playing in the attic. They cannot break through into the unusual stratum of sentience.

On such a day, for some reason, I seem to be unusually conscious of hidden impulses of thought, fear, and memory that fortunately have been buried within me. Suddenly I am prey to the recurrence of old hurts, guilts, regrets. Most of all, I am flooded by nostalgia, by the recall of matters that rise to the surface, causing small pains as acupuncture might, on this day, even if they never have before.

Next month I will be seventy-seven years old. I have lived
for almost twenty-five years with the same friend who hov-
ers about the edges of this day but plays no conspicuous
part in most of it, partly because she has grown tired of being written about, but mostly because my self-absorption
and egotism are so great that on this ordinary yet hypersensitive day I am only dimly conscious of her presence.
This accounts for the dominant (often inaccurate) appearance of the first-person singular pronoun.

Persons of an introverted stripe are solitary even when
they are in the presence of others. We are alone in a
crowd. In the one-act play I am recording here, I am the
only performer, even though such a day is densely popu-
lated with figures from memory and shades of the past. I
have observed that, when I am at work in the solitude of
my study, my best companions are those relatives, friends,
and acquaintances who live at a distance—and the dead.

I am beginning the seventh year of residence at the end
of a peninsula in down east Maine, looking out at a cove
that ultimately reaches the sea. I am prevented from
seeing wild water by the intervention of an island. I live
contentedly in a house that contains all I want of possessions. Myriad windows open out to everything I have any
desire for: woods, meadow, garden, water, shore, and the
sheltering sky.*

*A phrase I have borrowed from the title of Paul Bowles's memorable
novel.

I could, surely, put such a sensitive day behind me without recording it anywhere. Or I might ride it out, feeling much like the horseman in Albert Ryder's painting *Death on a Pale Horse*, in which the white figure is carried forward on the back of a white horse, unable to stop and unwilling to be distracted from its mortal mission.*

Or, as I have done here, I can keep a log of what happens this day, what I think and read, hear and remember. At times (thinking this is only fair to the reader) I decide to put away and not record things too terrible to dwell upon, only to discover by evening that they have returned, refusing to be unseated from the memory, clinging to growing darkness like an undislodgeable leech.

Perhaps the reader may think that such diurnal material is more suitable for a notebook one does not intend to look into again. It may be so. But in my life in this day the smallest matters seem to loom large, of a size with the greater recollections that are recorded in small, fine writing in my notes in order to diminish their effect. The frame of a day spent in one place, paradoxically, seems to raise the significance of everything without distinction.

No scale of values exists in such a day. In eighteen hours, everything is compressed by the limits of time. Only the tone in which one lives separates one occurrence

---

* This frightening picture hangs in the Cleveland Museum of Art. It may hang in other places as well because, I have been told, it is the most often forged work in American painting. Is it also the source of Katherine Anne Porter's title *Pale Horse, Pale Rider*?

from another. At breakfast my intentions for the day
ahead may be heavy with dread. But fortunately, the sight
of a doe coming out of the woods at noon may give
lightness to my lunch and, when it disappears, I will feel
free to take a nap. At night, the creak of a board upstairs
while I sit in a chair downstairs could be an occasion for
the return of apprehension. Small events create moods,
and others eradicate them, inexplicably.

I lie in bed, the shade of the window facing the cove pulled
up so I can catch the first appearance of the sun's light, a
hint of red at the bottom of a dark sky. No real light has
yet arrived. On some cold spring mornings I get up before
this—it is now 4:34—but today the room is agreeably
cool. Under the quilt it is warm. So I am seduced into lying still, my arms under my head, my eyelids fighting to be
lowered into sleep.

I begin to rehearse a catalogue of dread matters and
fears for the day ahead, an exercise I have indulged in
every morning of my adult life before I get up. (Of course,
it is also true that this dire review often takes place at a
worse hour—two o'clock in the morning—when I am unable to sleep.) During this dawn I cannot remember if I
ground the new Costa Rican coffee beans last night while
I was drying the dishes. I *did* dry the dishes, I can remember *that*, but what about the coffee beans? Dismay moves
from my chest to my eyes, which close at the thought that
there will be a disastrous delay before I can begin to drink

the life-saving, energy-raising brown beverage that should almost be served through an IV to start my day.

The window still shows nothing but black, with the small intervention of a distant light across the cove and its reflection in the water. Should I wait for some sign of daylight? I consider violating my old prescription for getting up. Then I remember that I once decided to call a memoir *Staying Put*. Today, for some reason, this makes me laugh. I throw off the warm covers, roused to action by amusement. I will stay put no longer. Staying put: how foolish that sounds. Once I looked up its origin in Eric Partridge* who informed me that it was a colloquial American expression thought by John Bartlett in the nineteenth century to be "a vulgar expression."

In darkness I leave the bedroom and come to the stairs. *Do not fall down them*, I instruct myself. I turn on the overhead light and look closely at the rawhide cords on my slippers to be certain they are tied. *Don't fall down the stairs*, I say to myself again and grip the rail. In my youth I used to race downstairs two steps at a time. Recently, I have had a recurrent dream in which I do this without my feet touching any of the steps and only my hand on the railing anchoring me to the staircase. Without that I might have flown. Now I go down in very slow stages, stopping often

* *A Dictionary of Slang and Unconventional English*, a most useful book. There *is* a book with this title, an editor later reminds me, by Scott Russell Sanders, published by Beacon Press in 1993.

and feeling very much like the figure in Duchamps's cubist painting,[*] except of course that I am fully clothed.

The time will come when it is no longer possible to make this safe descent. Then I plan to take up residence in the newly built room, which now we call the library. Its true name, a subtext to the present state of things—an ample spread of couches, oriental rugs, bookcases, and musical appliances—is the infirmary.

I turn the lights on in the living room and the kitchen, providing me with protection against the early-morning dimness. My ritual in the kitchen is as unvarying as a church rite: check the thermometer, fetch *The Book of Common Prayer*, fill the glass bottom of the coffeemaker with cold water and its mesh cradle with ground coffee. Here I offer a small orison of thanksgiving that I *did* grind the beans last night. Press the "on" button (do not laugh— sometimes I have set up the whole mechanism and waited for results before I found I had *not* pressed the button), go to the refrigerator for two slices of rye bread, margarine, orange juice, and skim milk, and set the toaster going.

There is more to this unvarying ritual. I put a spreader and a plate (my favorite, eight-sided Royal Staffordshire plate, the only one of this make I have, which I bought for 25 cents at a yard sale and which says "dishwasher safe" on the back) at my place, pour milk into a tiny pitcher of which I am foolishly fond and which holds exactly enough

[*] Known to the reader, of course, as *Nude Descending a Staircase*, which hangs in the Philadelphia Museum of Art.

liquid for two mugs of coffee, and add juice to a small green glass to which I am equally attached; none of these pieces has any value whatever, except to me.

I pour the hot, fragrant coffee, which always smells better than it tastes, although its effect is unmistakable. I bring everything to the table and sit down, gratefully, at my accustomed place where I get the widest possible view of the sunrise when it comes. I lighten the coffee with milk and put two tablets of NutraSweet into it, and then realize I have forgotten a spoon with which to stir it.

Rats! as my children used to say. Despite my devotion to the ceremony I have established with such care, I seem always to forget *something*, proving, I suppose, that there are holes in an aging memory that nothing, no amount of planning, will plug up.

I fetch the spoon, sit down again, stir, and open to page 41 of *The Book of Common Prayer* and begin to read aloud: "Dearly beloved, we have come together in the presence of Almighty God, our heavenly Father . . ." Then I stop, take a long drink of coffee and a mouthful of toast, and begin again. I paraphrase the introduction to the confiteor as I do precisely at this point every morning because I remember I am alone. I delete the first two words, and begin again: "I have come here . . ." By "here" (in place of "together") I mean "at the table in the kitchen in sight of the cove," my cherished place. Then I change the pronoun to "my" heavenly Father.

With no further false starts, I proceed to confess my

sins, relishing the sound of whole sentences and partial phrases for their literary elegance: "I have erred and strayed from thy ways like a lost sheep," and "I have left undone those things which I ought to have done, and I have done those things which I ought not to have done."

Nowhere in the *Book* do prayers appear to be written in the first-person singular. It assumes that we will all be praying together. Yet, for me, the most honest and satisfying prayer is private prayer, petitions and thanksgivings undisturbed by communal risings and kneelings, by the scrape and movements of others, the adult coughs and sneezes, the cries of babies across the aisle. In early morning solitude, filled with the freshness of the new day, and the energy a long, dark, silent night has pumped into me, I pray to a quiet, attentive God, with the pronouns of the text changed and the confidence that being alone has given me.

I drink orange juice* and two mugs of coffee, eating marmaladed toast as I make my way through the prescribed prayers, brushing away crumbs from the gutter of the *Book* and regretting the growing number of oily spots in the margins. Prayers are part of my breakfast; over the years I have liberally bestowed their pages with bits of other nourishment.

I push the chair back, close the book and stare at the pot of oxalis that stands on the table between my plate and the

---

* "Not from concentrate," the carton says. I like this phrase because it reminds me of the way my ideas come to me.

window. I look up to see the light begin to fill the sky. It moves slowly from the horizon into the bowl of darkness above Deer Isle. In that moment, the clover-shaped leaves of the oxalis, folded during the night into prayer-like postures, have opened into three-leafed flowers. Once again I have missed the action.

In this single pot of red leaves and tiny lavender blooms, I am able to see a whole garden, an entire border of flowers, an enormous bed of every variety. To me, this pot of oxalis is a distillation, a representative (as in the theory of democracy) of a huge constituency of blossoms. This morning, like every other morning in this kitchen for a long time, I recite into the caffeine-scented air:

> *To see the world in a grain of sand,*
> *And a heaven in a wild flower;*
> *Hold infinity in the palm of your hand,*
> *And eternity in an hour.*✦

Is it age, I wonder, that makes me enjoy reduction in almost every aspect of my life? I remember this began one autumn when I discovered a beautiful, changing maple on Rittenhouse Street behind our house in Barnaby Woods in the District of Columbia. It made me wonder why, years ago, my husband always drove our family to Vermont to see the color, the mile after mile of woods full of turning leaves. Was there not one tree in New Balti-

---

✦ William Blake, "Auguries of Innocence."

more (the village near Albany in which we then lived) that contained within its height and amplitude everything that the whole Granite State could offer to the traveler who had driven fifty miles to witness?

Eternity in an hour. I have become a minimalist of experience. Once I thought I could never travel to all the places I wanted to see, but in old age, the cove, in the variety of its seasons and weathers and times, seems to satisfy my need for new sights.

Infinity in the palm of your hand. Yesterday afternoon, listening to music in the new room, I thought about how my musical taste has suffered a similar sea-change. Season after season in the old Met, called by one contemporary critic "the yellow-brick brewery," I went to hear *Der Ring des Nibelungen.* I wallowed (is that too denigratory a word?) in the vast, lush, overwrought score, the wordy, rich libretto, the larger-than-life, huge-voiced singers and the garish sets (or what I could see of them from the side of the family circle).

Then under the influence of conductor John Barbirolli and cheap, standing-room tickets to the New York Philharmonic, I began to prefer symphonies and concerti, still on the opulent side of music, but without grand opera decor. In middle age I found I had become fond of chamber music, and in the last few years, listening to a recording of Glenn Gould performing his extraordinary, second version of *The Goldberg Variations*, I realized that I have again switched my allegiance. Now I prefer the variety, the ample swell and sweet decline, the abundant tones of a single instrument. *The world in a grain of sand.* Now there is no further retreat possible, except into that antithesis of music: silence. Like everyone else, of course, I will come to that.

The sun is up, and out. It strikes into my eyes, so I have to move my chair away from the view of the cove. I want to read in comfort and watch the finches arrive for breakfast at the two feeders. They are interesting creatures, the only ones who have stayed on faithfully through the cold of winter, with the exception of huge, hardy blackbirds and occasional chickadees. Last year at this time, or a little earlier, I witnessed the astonishing appearance of an evening grosbeak, a member of the finch family, but larger, showier, and alone, without its usual flock. It was a shock, like seeing a visitor from Mars coming across the meadow.

But the finches: At first, having given them only cursory glances at odd times, they seemed simply a flock of similar birds, differing in color (gold and purple in the ones that come here), but not in character.

Watching steadily this morning as they eat, I see I was wrong about their natures. One dictatorial-minded finch takes up a station at the end of the feeder and eats away stolidly, turning only to drop the husk of a sunflower seed to the ground. A fellow finch approaches and tries to settle at the other end of the rod. Furious, the first one flutters its wings ominously, seems to expand its entire narrow self, and then flies violently at the intruder, chasing it away.

This offensive tactic is repeated with each new arrival. For a minute or two, the bully has sole possession of the feeder, even though he has ceased to eat. Even satiated (I assume), the arrogant ruler of the hill does not move. No other challenger arrives. Triumphantly, the feeder's commander sits still until *I* can no longer bear it: I go to the window and rap loudly on the glass. The king abdicates. Not waiting for a sequel to the saga, I turn away from the window, having decided to settle into the relative peace of a book.

Beside my place at the breakfast table is a small stack of books I am in the process of reading, a place marker in each. I have begun them all at about the same time, deciding early each morning which one suits my need.

This is the first station ("base camp" might be another name for the place) at which sits my current reading. Base Camp Two is beside the comfortable chair in the living room. Three is on the high wicker stand in the bathroom to occupy my time and attention while I perform the usual daily chore. The fourth is on a table beside the couch in the library, and the last is upstairs beside my bed. There *is* a sixth, I remember now, in a wicker basket in the upstairs bathroom near the toilet, but since I rarely use that room, the books stay put (I see I have developed a fondness for this phrase now that I am somewhat informed about it) for months at a time, waiting to be opened, read, and finished.

I clear the dishes from breakfast to make room for the galleys of a thick collection of letters that Rachel Carson wrote to her friend Dorothy Freeman during the last twelve years of her life.* *The New York Times* sent them to me for review. I am rereading them slowly, taking notes in my usual fashion on the backs of envelopes although the review is long since published and there is little need for the notes. Once again I am aware that letters like these often provide a truer portrait of their writer than a biography might.

In the warm first sun of the day, I think about this. *Why?* I wonder. It may be because the constant, defining voice heard in letters is that of the writer/subject, not that of the biographer. There is no intrusive paraphrasing, no interpretation, only the explanatory notes of the editor, in this case, Martha, the granddaughter of Dorothy Freeman, to whom the letters were left. I find I trust the gentle, humble, selfless letters of Carson, her accounts of the terrible trials of her life, which she tries gallantly to play down, and most of all, her open declarations to Dorothy of her love.

I think of the premature interview—premature in that the book was not to be published for another month—given by Martha to an inquisitive radio interviewer. She

* *Always, Rachel*, published by Beacon Press in 1995.

asked why Rachel wrote two kinds of letters to Dorothy, some meant for her eyes alone and others intended for her husband to read. In one private letter, why did Dorothy celebrate one brief meeting by saying how lovely it had been to hang her clothes in the same closet as Rachel's? What did all this suggest?

Martha replied that the romantic tone of the letters, describing avid and carefully arranged trysts which were lovingly recalled afterwards, was inspired by their delight in having enough time together to *talk* more fully about matters of interest to them both.

There are very few letters from Dorothy in this selection. And what there are do not reveal very much of her person, probably because she is writing out of the caution born of a seemingly happy marriage and the presence of family. Or perhaps, I consider this morning, because she is not a writer gifted like Carson with the power to convey a true sense of herself even in almost daily letters.

I read a section and, as I reach to put the galleys down, I see on top of the pile a new book—a biography of the celebrated Maine writer Sarah Orne Jewett—just sent to me by Merloyd Lawrence, under whose imprint it appeared. At once, my plan for early morning breaks down. I sit with the new biography, interested in it because two years ago I reviewed a very poor work on the same subject which, I note, is properly not included in Blanchard's bibliography. I come to the paragraph that begins:

> The fact that Sarah Orne Jewett's deepest affections were always centered on women has naturally led to the question of whether she was lesbian. I believe she was not, in the strictest sense of the term. . . . [Her] love for other women was as passionate and absorbing as any heterosexual man's, but from all available evidence it never led to direct sexual expression.[*]

The biographer's assumption is based on her acceptance (in the same paragraph) of Carol Smith-Rosenberg's view[**] that in the nineteenth century women had romantic attachments and emotional interactions that were sexually normal (that is, heterosexual and without sexual hanky-panky), and in no way "deviant."

The sun is higher and stronger. Reading in the kitchen is now difficult. I need to move away. I close Jewett's biography and return it to its secondary place in the stack. I shut my eyes against the growing heat and sit, thinking about the need of so many people to answer in the negative the disturbing question: Were they lesbians? And to state their denial with such certainty.

Of course, *I* have no way of knowing what the exact condition of these women's sexual involvement was, any more than Paula Blanchard or Martha Freeman knew for certain. Or Judith Roman, for that matter, who wrote a bi-

[*] By Paula Blanchard, published by Addison-Wesley in 1995.
[**] In *Disorderly Conduct*, Oxford University Press, 1985.

ography of Annie Fields,⁺ with whom Jewett had what was called a "Boston marriage." Roman assures the reader that Annie Fields's long, happy marriage to James Fields precluded a lesbian relationship in her widowhood. This appeared to Roman to be another romantic, sexless relationship.

I tell myself I cannot spend any more prime morning time on this curious bias of biographers. My predilection naturally is to see the facts provided as evidence to the contrary. For these biographers, only an explicit, written "confession" of what the women did in their bedrooms would constitute adequate proof that these women were lesbians, the only way in which the word, to their way of thinking, applies. But I know there are as many kinds of homosexual love as there are varieties of heterosexual preference.

On my way out of the kitchen I find myself smiling because I remember Virginia Woolf's cool description of the privacy that always (in her time) surrounded lesbian relationships. "It cannot be denied that when women get together . . . they are always careful to see that the doors are shut and that not a word of it gets into print."⁺⁺

I go into the downstairs bathroom to wash and dress, having left my clothes downstairs last night out of habit from the winter when it was warmer there to undress at night and dress in the morning. As I hang my nightgown

---

⁺ *Annie Adams Fields*, published by Indiana University Press in 1990.
⁺⁺ *Orlando*, her famous novel, with androgyny as one of its themes.

behind the door I notice for the first time that it is imprinted with black-faced sheep, hundreds of them, in an infinitely repeated pattern.

I delay putting on jeans and a sweater while I stare at the flannel sheep. I think of Mull, the Hebrides island, where, last April, we spent three days driving through fortunately empty roads. I say "fortunately" because every road on the island is a single lane, both for coming and for going.

The hazards of such roads (of course there were others: driving on the left side of every Scottish road, and the long-forgotten skill of managing a manual-shift car) were only part of the nerve-wracking travel. From Craignure, where the ferry from coastal Oban landed, the single, slender road was thickly inhabited by numerous nonhuman occupants: sheep.

We crept along, very carefully. We went through mountains, forested glens, and bare cliffs and once stopped abruptly: A little convention of ewes was being held in the middle of the road, their spacious white backsides facing us. The small offspring of their fall mating with invisible rams (for this gathering at least), tiny spring lambs, nestled in among their ample mothers.

Sybil, my companion, decided the ladies were having their elevenses and would not move until they were quite finished. I suggested she blow the horn, but she refused to disturb the cozy confab. We sat. And sat. Then one ewe turned her head, saw us there, told the others (I assume, but we heard nothing in our closed car) who then turned to in-spect us. Slowly, *very* slowly they turned to the right, some to the left. Nudging their offspring ahead of them, they moved to the sides of the road. We were now free to move on, and we did, inching along so as not to frighten one of the skittish children back onto the road.

Sybil was wrong about the tea-time gathering. At every hour—morning, afternoon, and early evening—we were stopped in our progress by congenial assemblies of sheep on the roads. Later, at the inn where we stayed the night, run by a kilted laird and his wife, we were told that sheep had replaced cattle on Mull in the nineteenth cen-tury. Fertile grazing pastures had disappeared. The High-land moors lost their green color and turned brown. The human population dropped by eighty-five percent, and the island was left to the sheep (too many of them, the laird thought), who used the roads for their meeting halls.

Travel memories sometimes fill the dull spaces I need for daily tasks. This morning I shower, dry, powder, dress, brush my teeth, comb my hair, and file a broken nail, all the while sitting in the car on the blocked Mull road, watching the muster of sheep that had arrived in the bath-room by way of my imprinted nightgown.

It is almost seven. For all intents and purposes, I should be ready to go to work. I open all the doors to the house to bring in the morning cool, regretting in a way that I no longer have to perform the delaying work, the welcome distraction, of making a fire in the woodstove.

I glance at my desk and the hooded computer and printer, bestowing on them my serious intention to join them. But then, as usual, I think of something important to do in another room: Water the plants in the bay window of the new room. I see at once that I cannot do this for the can is empty. I take it to the kitchen and fill it with a squirt of liquid fertilizer and room-temperature water. Oh, the fine, dilatory pleasure of examining each geranium, amaryllis, ivy, oxalis, cactus, leftover Christmas poinsettia, for dryness. I water until the can is once again empty. I refold the throw rug on the couch from yesterday's nap, making sure the ends come together perfectly. *Now* I can go to work.

Well, almost. I turn on the radio to the local classical music station (by noon, constant talk takes over so Maine Public Radio is useful to me only in four morning hours and again in the evening) and hear the announcer say he will play some bel canto arias sung by, he says hesitantly, searching for the name of the soprano, "Uh, Lily Pons." He pauses. I can visualize him shaking his young head. Then I hear him say: "Yes, it says Lily Pons. I've never heard of her. It sounds more like a fancy kind of soap."

Oh my. I lean back in my chair and listen, remembering the late afternoon I accompanied my friend Woodie

Crohn (we were both in college at the time, I believe) to visit a wealthy, middle-aged chap who had a duplex apartment in New York in the east sixties. He greeted us at the door wearing an elegant maroon smoking jacket, black satin trousers that flared at the bottom, and leather sandals, his graying hair pulled back into a ponytail—a hairdo I had never before seen a man sporting, except in Western movies.

Woodie greeted him and started to introduce me. Our host put his finger to his lips and stopped us on the little iron balcony that looked down many feet to a living room as large as a ballroom. I became aware that all that great space was filled with music, the bell-like soprano sounds of *Lakmé*.

"The divine Lily," he whispered. Woodie nodded, clearly having recognized the voice at once. I nodded too, to be "in" on the identification, although I had no idea who the singer was.

Silently we were provided with bulbous glasses of wine. We sat in sling chairs facing an enormous Capehart Victrola, staring at its webbed speakers and opened mahogany top as though we expected the divine Lily to step out of it. We listened to the end of that record, another dropped down with a clatter upon it—it was *Un bel di vedremo*—and then another and another. Behind the Victrola I made out the printing on the brown backs of shelves of albums: Pons.

This was my first encounter with automatic changers. I

was astonished that our host (I have forgotten his name) did not have to get up to change records. During the short intervals, while the arm swept the completed record away and another dropped down, I expected him to speak. As I recall, he never did. We drank more wine, he put another stack of records on the spindle, we listened to more of Lily Pons's arias, until the sky at the top of the floor-length windows had turned dark blue. Lily sang on, our host's eyes closed against what I surmised he found the wondrous beauty of that voice.

Woodie and I had a date to meet his father for dinner. He stood up, I followed, he waved to the totally absorbed host. I did the same. He did not seem to be aware of our defection. We tiptoed up the iron steps and let ourselves out to the elevator's foyer. Behind the apartment door I could hear Lucia's *Sparsa e di Rose*.

"A fancy kind of soap," indeed.

I choose my reading matter for my time attending to eliminatory matters. My selection is a paperback of E. Annie Proulx's short stories, written before her little masterpiece *Shipping News* and her lesser, first, but still notable *Postcards*. I read a first-rate story, "Electric Arrows," so good that I stay longer than I need to on the toilet. Proulx writes of rural New Hampshire, which in most ways is much like rural Maine.

The story is about the tragic contrast between the lives of a poverty-stricken native family—the Clews—and a well-to-do summer couple—the Moon-Azures—who are from "away," as the local folk say. They have bought some of the natives' property, where they stay for a few months in summer; they winter in Florida. They have renovated the house in which old Mason Clew, the narrator of the story, was born.

I find this tale painful: *we* live on land that once belonged to Kenny Grindle. We live in his mother's now-restored house. He now lives in a camp across the road, his small piece of land filled with old bottles and wheels for sale, wood for his stove and, at the back, his clothes hang irregularly on a line.

We often give him rides to the post office or the general store. He asks us how business is in the bookstore or how my book is coming along. His favorite question is: How long does it take you to write one? But after reading "Electric Arrows," I wonder what he is really thinking: How stupid we are about the ordinary matters of country life? How did it come about that we look out our restored windows at the sea while he, who may have been born in our place, sees only passing trucks and tourists' cars coming down from Blue Hill to the Deer Isle Bridge? Does he ever wonder how his life came to be given to us? What has made us worthy to live here—what besides money and luck?

The Proulx short story has a good ending. Here and there in the tale, we have been told that the narrator's father, in idle moments during his lunch breaks, chiseled a primitive self-portrait into a granite stone behind his house. The last we see of the Moon-Azures, they have told a newspaper (and Mason is shown the story and picture by a neighbor) that they have found Indian carvings in rocks behind their house, "complex petroglyphs such as the recently discovered Thunder God pictured here . . . rare among the eastern woodland tribes." The friend says, "Didn't know there was no Indians around here." The narrator laughs, finding it very funny that his father's figure, cut into the field rock during long summer noons half a century ago, is now mistaken for an archeological find.

Oblivious, often pretentious, wealthy people try to buy the family photos of the Clews who now live in the hired man's old house. Wiser natives, people full of humor who once belonged to these places, have been displaced because their orchards failed (oh my, *we* have the remains of an apple orchard on *our* place) and so they needed to sell off their old place bit by bit.

I put the book of stories* at the bottom of the bathroom stack, determined, for the moment, to read no more of these accurate, skillful, affecting tales. I swish mouthwash around my clenched teeth, still dwelling on Mason Clew

* *Heart Songs and Other Stories.* The paperback edition I am reading is from Scribner Paperback Fiction, Simon & Schuster, and came out last year, 1995.

who lives with Reba, his wife, and his aunt, who mourns that "properties break apart." And Mason's recognition of the mistaken illusion the new people have that "country life makes you good."

The sun pours into the living room, now sadly denuded of its couches and sideboard, which have been moved to furnish the new room. I sit in the ugly but comfortable brown chair, trying to persuade myself to take the short walk into my study to begin work. *Now,* I tell myself, watching the finches fight it out over fully occupied perches on the feeder, and looking longingly at *Heart Songs* because one good story, like one olive, awakens a taste for another, and deciding I am thirsty and need a glass of ice water before I venture into the no man's land that is my study to sit before the reproachful silence of my computer's keyboard and printer.

Finally, I get to my feet, resolved to let nothing—even the profound thirst I imagine grips me—stop me from entering the war zone. I look out at the cove one last time and see that the light has filled the whole bowl of sky, that there is no obstacle of fog or haze to block my view of the blue strip that is Deer Isle, that the meadow is green and full of wild flowers about to be cut down by a ruthless mower. All this I noticed yesterday, and the day before for that matter, but I take careful note of it again today because such careful observation keeps me from making the move towards work.

My customary next stop is at Base Camp 2 ½, the desk that faces the cove, not at the summit that is the computer. I recognize, of course, that this is yet another delaying action, and yet . . .

Set squarely at the center of my desk pad is a copy of one of Somerset Maugham's novels, with a piece of toilet paper marking my place. I brought it in here yesterday from the bathroom. Why? Yes, now I see why. I wanted to remember something Maugham says:

> Sometimes a man hits upon a place to which he mysteriously feels he belongs. Here is the home he sought, and he will settle amid scenes that he has never seen before, among men he has never known, as though they were familiar to him from his birth. Here at last he finds rest. [*]

I see that I have begun to collect explanations for why I feel I belong in this place, why I have no desire to leave it even for a short vacation or visit, why I resist accepting invitations to sign books, to "appear" or read or make speeches "away," as ego-gratifying as those activities are.

I was born and raised in the heart of a great city. In my later years I went on living in cities or in areas very close to cities. Now, in this place, are scenes I have never looked on before, although occasionally I stayed for short summer periods close to the ocean. Always, I was awed by its wildness or becalming flatness, its infinite stretch.

[*] *The Moon and Sixpence*, 1919, the Doubleday Doran edition.

The cove is hardly ocean, but instead a *reductio* of it, a little spit of it, a satisfactory sample, corseted by visible shores and ending in a narrow strip of distant land, an horizon marked off more in watercolors than in the firmness of oils. Once again I see I have settled happily for what I have been given—restricted landscape, the bare essentials of extent and expanse. The cove is a minimalist's delight, of limited scope but, within its restricted boundaries, of infinitely varied views that never repeat themselves.

Now it is eight-thirty, an hour later than the time I have targeted to sit at this desk. The time has been spent avoiding the mail and the bills, and the real work, fiction. The computer's chair, which faces a wall, not the water, and therefore does not distract me with what I really prefer to look at, has not budged an inch from its empty, pushed-in position.

First I decide to tackle the mail piled in the center of the desk. Most of it I answer with a postcard, thanking the writers for taking the time and trouble to say something about my books. But some letters are so good, so thoughtful that I put them in a separate place to answer at some length. This pile has grown to gratifying proportions.

Here on top is a letter from a woman who now lives alone in Moody, Maine, a place on the southern coast familiar to me for many summers. As I read her moving letter, I can visualize the enormous expanse of Moody Beach at low tide, so vast that the eye has no place to rest at its end, no terminus, no *surroundings* to its white sand and un-ending water.

She writes that she felt a kinship with my last book, "having fled an unhappy marriage of many years to live . . . within sound, if not sight, of the ocean." She describes her occasional exhilaration at being alone, at times feeling liberated and productive (as a writer), at other times terrible, when she experiences a "death of the spirit," aware of her psychic and physical imperfections. She wonders "who would ever love or live with this person again. . . . And the fear that as I search for myself I will find something—or nothing."

The rest of her letter is equally poignant. What I have written about contentment at being alone for six weeks does not reflect her experience (or that of some of my other correspondents). Her response is bitter: "I only wish that, like you, I was assured of an end to this solitude." She writes an anguished confession of unfulfilled dreams, weakness, loneliness, a sense of wasted life.

I do not know how to respond adequately. Hers is only the last in a series of such letters to me, a sign of the effect on others of the published word, I suppose, but equally a testimony to my unpreparedness to deal with the lives of others. I had thought the memoir was individual and personal, but some readers see it as a prototype of parts of their lives and wish to add their painful details to mine. This correspondent deserves a more complete reply than I have time to give. I have been unjust in *Fifty Days*, calling forth outpourings of autobiography without providing for an adequate vessel to catch them in, inviting responses, and yet preparing no comforting words to respond to them.

I write a sparse, unsatisfactory postcard to the woman who lives in Moody.

After a few more cursory postcards, I reach for a full sheet of stationery to write to Helen Yglesias, my friend who has been gone for the winter from this cold and inhospitable (to her arthritis) place to New York and then to Florida. In the city she stays in a residence house for women at which she has breakfast and dinner and from whose permanent residents she hears life stories that are "endlessly engrossing," she writes.

I miss her. She has been away from Maine for a month. Her letters are full of her sadness—a very sick, ninety-year-old sister, a cancer-afflicted ex-husband. Saddest of all from one point of view (mine, I suppose), she says there's a book in all this experience, the residents and her family, "but I'm beginning to think my book-writing days are over. I've lost the energy, the ego, the hope that it matters."

Age and a growing list of disabling ailments will do this to some good writers. My friend has written four first-rate books, two of them best sellers, numerous reviews, and served as literary editor of *The Nation*. But with her fifth book she has suffered all the slings and arrows of outrageous fortune, which found no publishers willing to take a chance on one she says is "very political." I have not read it because she has not shown it to me.

Rejection is an affliction as painful as shingles or loss of a limb, or for that matter a review which I am bracing myself for when the mail comes today. It brings on a terrible case of terminal self-doubt. No matter how many acceptances and how much critical approval precede it, the ego—that staunch backbone that holds up all writers—fails any longer to assure you that what you write has value, or that you have found a unique way of saying it. Osteoporosis of the will sets in and, like my friend, the failure of "the hope that it matters" kills off the desire to go on writing.

I sit, staring out the window at a squirrel I know is making his greedy way to the bird feeder, trying to think of something to write to Helen. Nothing comes. Shall I communicate my anxiety about the review I am expecting this morning? No. She has enough problems of her own. I decide to wait until tomorrow to answer her letter.

Under it is another letter that arrived yesterday from a garden-loving friend. She tells me that, after her slight stroke, she said to someone, "You know what a pachysandra I am," intending of course to say "Pollyanna." I laugh, and use the paper intended for Helen to tell my now-recovered friend how amusing I think that is.

It is nine. Carol will have the mail at the post office sorted by now. I have paid the oil bill and the snow-plowing bill and the electric bill, so I stow away the checkbook, noting that our joint account is down to what is aptly termed a bare minimum. I put the rest of the bills aside, gather up the mail to go, and find a sweater to wear for my trip "into town" to the post office. Early morning in late June up here still clings to the end of winter.

Sargentville's post office (it serves a winter population of fewer than a hundred persons and not too many more in summer) is in a single room the size of a walk-in closet, which is tucked into the side of a private house. It is a little more than a mile from our place. Many people walk to it. I, unsure of my footing and certain that one or another of the road-repair or delivery trucks will run over me, do not.

Our post office is an endangered species. In its uninformed wisdom, the postal service has decided to close it, along with more than thirty others around the state, "to save money." The residents are indignant. We are blessed with a postmistress, Carol, who is infinitely skilled in all the arcane operations of the postal service (my favorite oxymoron), but she is labeled "temporary," and has no benefits of any kind. Her value to residents is inestimable. She knows everything that goes on in our area: who is away (for whom she is holding mail), where those are who come for the summer and when they will be back, what mishaps have occurred on any road in our vicinity— everything, in short, that makes communal small-village life so interesting—and important.

Rather than wait for late afternoon rural mail delivery,

many people get to the post office soon after the mail is sorted, meet with each other, and exchange news, opinions, and information about the state of each other's health. My partner will be lost without these morning encounters. Knowing the state of affairs in the village and the problems or well-being of everyone who lives there, she can then retire to the seclusion of her bookstore with a sense that she has done her business with the outside world.

As for me, I am not gregarious and rarely visit the post office. But today Sybil is busy so I go for the mail, carrying my own and hoping I will not encounter anyone. Talk in the morning is hard for me, as is news on the radio. It knocks whatever literary plans I have out of my head, dissipating ideas I have decided to explore into the thin, cold air.

This day I am lucky. There is no one there but Carol who seems to know instinctively that I am untalkative this morning (like so many other mornings). She hands me a pack of mail, rubber-banded together, the dilatory folded *New York Times* at the bottom, says only, "Nice this morning," and then, "Bye now." I say, "Goodbye and thank you," rather a long utterance for me. I've decided not to visit the general store, a mile away, because, in riffling through the mail I spot a long envelope from W. W. Norton.

I know I need to fill my gas tank at the store. But my hand will shake too much to pump gas. I will spill it all over myself. I bury the Norton envelope deep into the bottom of the letter pile, and drive home.

Home is where there is no one at the moment, and there will be no noise. I open the door and am swept by gratitude for the silence.

I sit at the kitchen table and undo the elastic bands, sorting the mail into four piles: one for Sybil and Wayward Books, one for me, one for our mutual interests, and one for all the unwanted, never-to-be-opened solicitations, advertisements, catalogues, etc. I stare bleakly at my pile, still unable to face the envelope from Norton.

On top of yesterday's *Times* is the national weekly edition of the *Washington Post*, important to us because, despite our long separation from that city, we sometimes miss the news of its troubled local government as well as the canny reportage of national news. I go through it quickly and find that George Will, with whom I usually disagree, has an article on gays in the military. I cannot resist reading it (as I expected, we do not see eye to eye on this matter) before I chide myself for wasting time and go back to the pile.

There is the new *Consumer Reports*—this issue is about cordless phones. We have been debating whether or not to buy such an instrument for about two years, thinking how nice it would be not to have to take our old phone, with yards of wire attached to it, out on the deck when we are expecting a family member or a friend to call. Now we will be informed about the best one to buy *if* we can bring ourselves to spend the money.

And then there is a thick catalogue from the University of California Press for a sale of its backlist. I turn at once to the Mark Twain page and see that the Press is selling the second and third volumes of his letters, which I do not own in this new form, as well as a collection of his early writings. I turn the corner of the page down, resolved to order them.

I go into the new room to be sure I don't have any of these. The Twain collection now occupies ten shelves, from ceiling to floor of the built-in cases in the library. I own most of the inexpensive and easy-to-find volumes. So, like all collectors, I am faced with the need to spend a great deal of money for rarer volumes. But my interest in this collection is no longer as great as it was when I thought I might publish some of my iconoclastic views of that most iconoclastic writer.

I do not refer to this collection often. But the catalogue has stirred my acquisitive instincts. I begin to review the contents of a shelf and pull down a small volume, *The Wisdom of Mark Twain*,* that contains some fine, not-often-quoted wit. As I scan its pages I think how often his humor is disillusioned and darkly contemporary:

* Edited by Michael Joseph in 1970 for Stanyon Books and Random House.

The duel is one of the most dangerous institutions; since it is always fought in the open at daybreak, the combatants are sure to catch cold.

Everyone is a moon, and has a dark side which he never shows to anybody.

I have been complimented many times and they always embarrass me; I always feel they have not said enough.

Everything human is pathetic. The secret source of humor itself is not joy but sorrow.

Well, I suppose dueling is not modern, but then there are the cutting political remarks: "It could probably be shown by facts and figures that there is no distinctly native American criminal class except Congress," and in the same vein, "Fleas can be taught nearly everything that a Congressman can."

Scholars have spent decades culling bits and pieces of his wit from his books, letters, speeches, autobiographies, and biographies. I have five such volumes, all sitting together on a shelf. They are the ones I seem to go to most often, except for *Huckleberry Finn* and "The Man That Corrupted Hadleyburg," a story that haunts me for its black, accurate misanthropy.

When Twain condenses his observations about the human race into an epigram, wisdom that is more often found disseminated throughout long novels and stories, I like it best. This preference is another example, I suppose, of my affection for contraction, diminution, abridgment, curtailment.

Standing before these shelves is dangerous. I could spend the morning reinserting myself into one or another of these beloved books. After this first book of humor I move on to *Mark Twain Laughing*. But then I tell myself I cannot spend time this way, to no purpose, for no immediate use, for this self-indulgence.

Back to the kitchen table, and the mail.

I open a package that contains a very thick manuscript, sent from the associate publisher of Tilbury House in Gardiner, Maine. It turns out to be an anthology of quotations put together by ninety-year-old Helen Nearing, called *Light on Aging and Dying*. It is a coincidence that it arrived in today's mail, because I have just come from Twain's dark wisdom on the same subjects, most memorably: "All say, 'How hard it is that we have to die'—a strange complaint to come from the mouths of people who have had to live."*

I go through the pages quickly, and note that every quotation in Helen Nearing's manuscript is happy, content with age and aging, even pleased with it. Not one mentions the indignities of the condition. I decide I will write to the publisher who asks me for a blurb to tell her that nothing could be further from my far-less-cheery view of

---

* One of Pudd'nhead Wilson's maxims.

the subject. I will send her a contrasting selection of quotations, such as Golda Meir's "Old age is like a plane flying through a storm. Once you're aboard there's nothing you can do about it," and others in *my* private stock of pessimistic aphorisms.*

I open a number of third-class requests, from Planned Parenthood, the Democratic Party, the Whitman-Walker Clinic (for AIDS) in Washington, National Public Radio, NOW, and four other, lesser organizations and charities, asking for money. All are worthy, but I have responded to them recently, writing on my *one* yearly contribution to these places that I can afford only what I am sending at the present. I say I will send no more until next year at this time and add, "I would be grateful if you would save the very appreciable costs of printing and mailing further requests (sometimes they arrive a month after I have written a check), using the money for your primary purpose, not to solicit more funds, which I now inform you I am not able to send." (This response to my initial check always reminds me of the fisherman who has hooked one fish and, encouraged, goes on casting in the same spot for the rest of the day.)

Does my request succeed? Never. Not once. So I collect all the subsequent dunnings, together with catalogues for

---

* Soon after this manuscript left my hands, Helen Nearing died in an automobile accident at the age of ninety-one. In the light of her great optimism, her death was indeed premature.

clothes made for women half my size, for shoes with heels I have not worn for thirty years, for garden equipment to be used by persons with gardeners or money—probably both—and deposit all of it in the trash. Two days ago the basket was empty. Now it is full, with enough unwanted paper to reconstitute a tree.

There is one other package to open, a large one from Norton, my publisher. It contains pristine paperback copies of a book of mine that came out last year. I inspect them with the dismayed feeling I always have at such moments, my heart sinking at the realization that all the errors, variations, infelicities, and other literary sins committed during two years of work are now permanent, indeed they are cemented into irrevocable print, and there is nothing I can do about them.

Then I remember a story our friend and fellow bookseller Barbara Falk told me about the writer who learned that a bookstore on Fifth Avenue had a display of her new book that filled the whole window. Delighted, she took a cab to the store. As she got out, unable to resist, she said to the driver, "I wrote that book over there in the window."

"*All* of them?" he asked incredulously.

⁓

I return to the first-class mail. There is a short letter from Ed Kessler, the wittiest of my correspondents. He now lives in Boston and he writes: "Walking through the Public Gardens I heard a sort of punk type say (at the foot of the statue of George Washington) in response to 'Who's that?' from his companion: 'One of the old people who live on monuments.' "

Having read or inspected every single piece of mail, except the dreaded letter, and having opened every package and disposed of every catalogue, there is nothing for it. The moment of truth. I slit open the Norton envelope, and there it is, a photocopy of next Sunday's *Times* review of my novel, reduced in size, I quickly decide, because my considerate editor could not bear to have me see it in all the gore of full-sized print.

Recently, a novelist-acquaintance of mine received a rotten review, a thorough, out-and-out destruction of three years of her work, in this same paper. I was filled with pity for her, thinking I should send my condolences. But I lacked the courage, not knowing what to say in the face of such printed devastation. So I said nothing. Instead, like the egoist that all writers are, I retreated into a moment of silent prayer and fervent hope that the novel of mine due to appear soon would not be the object of similar treatment.

But now, as I should have expected it to happen at least once in a long career, here it is. I have joined my acquaintance in what I imagine was *her* fury, her despair, her self-pitying misery. The *Times*, in a two-column review that occupies an entire page, has effectively consigned my book to the ash heap, suggesting by implication that I am

Friends and Lovers

Doris Grumbach's novel tracks the painful progression of four disappointed lives.

THE BOOK OF KNOWLEDGE

By Doris Grumbach.
248 pp. New York:
W.W. Norton & Company. $22.

By Sara Maitland

THIS is a rather nasty book. I do not mean that Doris Grumbach's seventh novel, "The Book of Knowledge," is violent or obscene, but rather that it is small-minded, ungenerous. It is some- unsympathetic to the an-

the stuff of teen-age angst and self-knowing — but these four never recover, never grow up, never balance their aspirations with the joys of the real world. Lionel ends up dead, a war hero, and he is the lucky one; the rest end up defeated and foiled. Like the reader, they are given no insight and no hope.

The novel is frustrating: such a to-do about nothing. It is also frustrating because it is titillating: incest, homoeroticism (of both sexes), mystical fervor — all these are sexually charged, but Ms. Grumbach sets up these issues and then has nothing passionate or compassionate to say.

the most incompetent, insensitive, untalented writer ever to put pen to paper (an outdated image, I realize).

I have to sit down to absorb it all. Suddenly I am Twain's Person Sitting in Darkness, trying to conjure up some consolations. I remind myself of something I read recently, something that Saul Bellow told his biographer. Yes. It was that literature is no longer central to American life, that the novel itself has no importance. But these generalizations are hardly convincing under the full force of my reviewer's adjectives: my novel is "small-minded," "ungenerous," "unsympathetic," "lacking in compas-

41

sion," "very badly constructed," "clumsily paced," "dismal in tone," "leaden." All this in seven paragraphs.

The only interruption I can find to this litany of faults is a single half-sentence written by Sara Maitland, the reviewer, in a weak moment of her critical attack. She claims that "sentence by sentence the novel is very well written: sharp observations and crusty irony, quick changes of viewpoint and delicate shifts of tone." In the next sentence she weakens again and concedes to "skillful prose." This temporary softening makes me think of a totally untrained platoon sent into battle surrounded on all sides by teams of Green Berets.

I ask myself how a book could be, sentence by sentence, very well written and still be leaden, dismal in tone, etc. I can think of no satisfactory answer to this. Then I resort to some attempt at levity. I try to imagine a suitable illustration for this review, had the *Times* chosen to use one. I decide on Edvard Munch's lithograph *The Cry*, showing me graphically in my despair, "trembling with anxiety," as Munch said of the figure in a stark landscape, full of "inner turmoil."

But I can not maintain this humorous note for long. Instead, I go in search of a little book on my shelf that I remember contains an ample selection of other *Rotten Reviews*.* I see that some fine writers received very bad reviews for what turned out in time to be classic works. In a nineteenth-century magazine, the *Athenaeum*, Herman Melville was told that *Moby-Dick* was "so much trash . . . an ill-compounded mixture of romance and matter-of-fact," full of "errors" and "heroics." He was accused of being "disdainful of learning the craft of an artist."

Wuthering Heights, Emily Brontë's masterpiece, was dismissed at the time of its appearance as "a crude and morbid story," and a contemporary reviewer of *Our Mutual*

---

*All the quotations come from the collection put together by Bill Henderson for Pushcart Press in 1986.

Friend consigned Charles Dickens to an "inferior rank" among his fellow novelists. In 1855 a newspaper called Longfellow's *Hiawatha* "childish nonsense." And almost one hundred years later Virginia Woolf was told by a critic that *The Waves* was dull, and by another that *To the Lighthouse* "had all the weaknesses of poetry in it."

Somewhat mollified, I search for other historical consolations. Wordsworth's *The Prelude* in 1850 was termed an "endless wilderness of dull, flat, prosaic twaddle," and the *Athenaeum* let it be known to the English public that Oscar Wilde's *The Portrait of Dorian Gray* was "unmanly, sickening, vicious . . . and tedious."

And more ego assuagement—*Le Figaro*: "Monsieur Flaubert is not a writer"; *The Springfield Republican: The Great Gatsby* is "a little slack, a little soft, more than a little artificial. . . . [It] falls into the class of negligible novels."

I find myself absorbing these slams gratefully. I enjoy knowing that Samuel Johnson said he hardly knew "a more corrupt work" than *Tom Jones*. And that Thomas Carlyle thought Ralph Waldo Emerson "a hoary-headed and toothless baboon." And that Emerson himself dealt Jane Austen's novels a heavy blow by calling them "vulgar in tone, sterile in artistic invention, imprisoned in the wretched conventions of English society, and quite without genius."

There is no end to my consolations. An English journal decided Walt Whitman "is as unacquainted with art as a hog is with mathematics," Henry James wrote for *The Nation*'s readers that Whitman's attitude was "monstrous," and one Peter Bayne (in *Contemporary Review*) said he was "incapable of true poetic originality."

Gloomily, I think about quitting the practice of fiction altogether. I remember that Herman Melville received such rough treatment from the press for *Moby-Dick* that he stopped writing for forty years. Such stoppage would preclude any further words from me. But then I tell myself, perhaps it is better to be called "small-minded, ungenerous, unsympathetic," *und so weiter*, than to be compared to a hog or a baboon, or to be labeled obscene, contemptible, or corrupt.

I turn to the back of Bill Henderson's collection and try to ease my distress by reading the cynical quotations on the institution of reviewing, itself. I tell myself I should not take notice of these opinions since I have spent the last thirty-five years reviewing books. Still, I take some pleasure in learning that Anthony Burgess thinks the reviewers' profession "is more given to stupidity and malice and literary ignorance even than the profession of novelist," and that Sherwood Anderson shared Melville's view: "When a man publishes a book there are so many stupid things said that he declares he'll never do it again."

Nothing helps. I try to submerge myself in a sea of recriminations. I say: Sara Maitland must be hopelessly prejudiced against my subject matter—the terrible cost of

leading sexually closeted lives in the '30s. I refer to the review. No, this is not her motive. She does not touch upon
my theme at all. It must be she hates the way I write. No,
she says she likes that, in a way. I search my memory to see
if I ever reviewed *her* badly. No, nothing there. I have
never read her work. I have never even heard of her. She is
not being retributive.

Have we ever met, and did she take an instant and permanent dislike to me? No record of that, unfortunately.

I can think of no way of explaining her rotten review
except the worst explanation of all: it is just possible that
the reviewer is right—*it is truly a bad book*. But no writer,
no matter how cribbed and cosseted against criticism, can
entertain that dire thought for long.

As long as I have not been called "morally insane," as
Walt Whitman was termed after *Leaves of Grass* appeared,
or the novel was not labeled "sentimental rubbish," as
Anna Karenina was, I decide it is possible to carry my cloud
with me (like Charlie Brown's friend Pigpen) into my
study, and get to work on yet another book—this one.

I gather up the black-thumb review, the letters I will answer, the bills I will have to pay tomorrow morning (I'm
compulsive about paying them right after they arrive for
fear, someone once told me, I will die in the night and
leave behind the impression of being a deadbeat), a postcard from my friends Ted and Bob who are vacationing in

Mexico and send me a seductive view of the beautiful ce-
note, Dzitnup, we visited a few years ago, and the two-
day-old *New York Times*, the treasure of every morning.

It is almost ten. Filled with my customary morning guilt
and a sense of wasted time, I enter my study, fatalistically
carrying yesterday's *Times* with me. Before I sit at the
computer, I open the paper on my desk . . . to the obitu-
aries. Persons of a certain age will tell you, if they are honest, that this is the first page they turn to every day. Why?
To celebrate their own survival? Perhaps. But I do not feel
any pleasure in being alive in the presence of death notices. Instead, I notice that I read the name of the de-
ceased first and then, immediately, the age. If they were
younger than I, I mourn their premature "passing," as the
euphemism goes, but if they are older, I am encouraged:
perhaps I too . . .

This day, there are two vaguely worded death notices of
men in their thirties, suggesting that their carefully speci-
fied deaths from "lymphoma" and "cancer" may be eu-
phemisms. These men leave behind parents and siblings,
but usually no other family. I suspect this nomenclature is
the family's choice, but one never knows. A young fisherman on Deer Isle died of AIDS; his greatest fear was not
so much the disease as his friends' and neighbors' discov-
ery of the truth.

Then I read that three persons over eighty have died,

one over ninety, and another a year younger than I. Ordinarily, for me, longevity in the state of Maine is a comforting statistic. Still, death is the single terrible fact we cannot face at whatever age, although it is easier to contemplate these announcements than the thought of one's own.

Today I find my response to the obituary page confusing. For the moment, age does not matter. Every death, unless it is voluntary, is an inexplicable loss, an unwarranted assault upon the accumulated pleasures and experiences of life, a condition to be raged against (as Dylan Thomas urged his father to do).

I sympathize more with such raging, wild ravings, keenings, and violent hair- and clothes-tearing, the uncontrollable tears of mourners, than the "civilized," decorous, quiet, folk song–filled "celebrations of life" that are now offered in churches for the dead. So many modern requiems are described in this way: a celebration. What is there to celebrate, come to think of it, now that the principal celebrant can not be present and those who remain are usually filled with sorrow? Something very valuable is lost, gone for all eternity, out of the world, and to where? Fury, I think, is the only proper response.

To remove the bitter taste of death and the review from my head, I turn, as is my daily custom, to the crossword puzzle. There is something unchanging in my approach

Harry Kondoleon

1955–1994

Alfred • A • Knopf

to the newspaper; I go from one habitual page to the next, taking pleasure in the ritual. Peter deVries knew that "there is nothing more boring than unrelieved novelty."[*]

Before I can enter the first word I think I know, I see a large, black-bordered box that a publisher has placed just above the puzzle. It is in memory of an acquaintance, Harry Kondoleon, a talented playwright and novelist who died last week . . . of AIDS. I see now there is no way to escape news of death, even if I avoid the obituary page. This plague is bountiful and omnipresent, and I will come

---

[*] I have no idea where this observation comes from. I found it in my head.

upon news of its latest victim in other sections of the paper. I had heard that Harry was sick and had written to him; I did not know until this moment that he had died.

I stare at the empty squares of the puzzle, seeing in them the bright, airy, charming figure of Harry as he swept down Yaddo's wide staircase in the mansion on his first evening at the colony.

"They told me they dress for dinner here," he said. Of course, no one did, not since the retirement of Elizabeth Ames, the original doyen of the mansion. Harry was wearing a velvet dress with a train, his black hair flowing to his shoulders. At table he was full of witty rejoinders and bright observations, cheering the usually glum writers and painters (the composers were over at a corner table being glum by themselves) with his lovely costume and his sprightly conversation. He was a charming fellow and I always wanted to sit at his table for dinner.

Dead, at the unripe young age of thirty-nine, the same age that Dylan Thomas went ungentle into his own dark night:

Good men, the last wave by, crying how bright
Their frail deeds might have danced in a green bay,
Rage, rage against the dying of the light.

My interest in today's puzzle has waned. Finding Dylan Thomas in the memory bank of poems I have loved and learned causes me to move on to another title of his stored there: "In my craft or sullen art . . ." *My* craft waits on the

stand near the computer across the room, having been
dealt a severe blow by this morning's review. Sullen craft
it is today.

I don't get up to move to the corner where the computer
sits, smugly awaiting my presence, knowing so much more
than I do, such a show-off, so ready to go to work. I, on the
other hand, am immobilized, sunk in thinking about
Harry's death last week and Dylan's almost fifty years ago.

While I am working up the will to move, the telephone
rings. I think I will leave it to the answering machine in
the kitchen. But the insistent ring persuades me it may be
something important—or dire. Whenever I surrender to
the temptation to answer the telephone it is because, after
a struggle, I have convinced myself that grave tidings
await me at the other end, never good news or matters of
interest. To me, the phone is like the radio and the television, dangerous to my peace of mind in that they all instantly transmit portentous events. Only the newspaper,
by its delayed arrival, is a bearable purveyor of terrible
happenings.

I say "hello" to an editor at a magazine called *Allure*
who, months ago, had asked me to write a piece for her on
my elderly opinions about beauty and fashion. At the
time, I was ignorant of the existence of the magazine. She
described it to me. Now she wishes to send me copies of
the magazine in which the essay appears. I had told her
that my views were most likely to be both retrogressive
and iconoclastic, that neither she nor her beautiful young

readers would care for them at all. I said the elderly were often unconcerned about beauty and fashion because most of them were invisible. They grew to look alike as they aged, at least to the young. "If they've seen one, they've seen 'em all," I told her.

Strangely enough, she liked the piece I wrote, sent me a generous (to my mind) check for it, and then called again to ask when a Boston photographer could come up to take my picture. I told her I had a photograph from the jacket of my last book. "Oh, no," she said, "we need one of our own."

I despise being photographed. It is a matter of extreme ego, of not wanting to be reminded of what I now look like, of not wanting others to see the ravaged self. But the editor insisted, so we made an arrangement for that. Then, to my horror, she asked if she could also send someone to do my makeup and hair for the photograph. I was horrified because I had written (and she had read) in my little screed that the elderly stop caring very much about such matters. Never seen as individuals, they believe such efforts on themselves are quite useless.

My piece was about sameness: gray or white hair, wrinkled skin, false teeth that look too new for old faces, curved backs, blotched hands, unsure feet. Their clothes are indistinguishable, differing only slightly according to climate in various parts of the country. As politely as I could, I said no, don't send up any such person. I would do whatever needed to be done, which of course consisted

mainly in combing my hair and avoiding all useless appli-
cations of makeup.

I hung up and went through a rapid self-examination
about the whole affair. Why did I agree to write it in the
first place? Why did I agree to the photography thing?
What will I do when the photographer arrives? Maybe I
will be dead by then, the usual way I have of dealing with
unpleasant future events. Then I remembered the generous check and called to make an appointment for a
haircut.

This morning I say, "Thank you," hang up, and shudder at the whole enterprise.

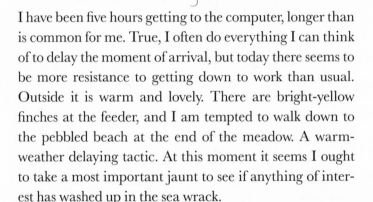

I have been five hours getting to the computer, longer than
is common for me. True, I often do everything I can think
of to delay the moment of arrival, but today there seems to
be more resistance to getting down to work than usual.
Outside it is warm and lovely. There are bright-yellow
finches at the feeder, and I am tempted to walk down to
the pebbled beach at the end of the meadow. A warm-
weather delaying tactic. At this moment it seems I ought
to take a most important jaunt to see if anything of interest has washed up in the sea wrack.

Once, years ago on our beach, we found a *whole* china
soap dish (I think it was, but it may have been a butter
dish), in which we now store a motley collection of keys,
bag twisters, and coins. No one to whom we show it will
believe we found it where we did and in that perfect, un-

chipped condition. So encouraged, we now go down often to search, finding of course only broken pieces of crockery among the mounds of broken glass. Sybil rejects these bits; she is hoping to find enough matching shards to complete a full, twelve-piece table setting.

I take my cane and walk to the shore.

Ten-thirty. Finally I am seated in the "amen corner"[*] of the study. Having resolutely turned my back on the seductive cove for purposes of work, I now look out at nothing but the wall containing framed broadsides of quotations from, and woodcuts of, Eric Gill, Walt Whitman, and Ben Shahn—and closer, at the gray, blank display screen. I attach three new manuscript pages to a standup clipboard, turn on the infernal machine, and call up a file. Then I sit, glaring at the screen and the silent keyboard that is superciliously awaiting instructions, for what is called my "input."

In my scrabbly handwriting, the manuscript pages take on the look of reality. The few typed lines I have now called up on the screen, the work of yesterday morning, do not. Handwritten manuscript (is that not a redundancy?) is an extension of the self, the scratched-out, inserted-over, raffish, uneven scrawl that is part of my hand and, ultimately, my brain. But the screen holds something that re-

[*] Called this, by me, because of the finality of the computer to my literary enterprises. In some Protestant churches one side of the pews is assigned the pronouncement of "amen" at the end of prayers.

sembles an artificial translation, the product of a machine. For all I know, with all signs of a human agent absent, these seemingly finished, completed words might have been produced by an intelligent baboon (*that* again) or a well-instructed robot.

My view of this machine is idiosyncratic. It seems to me it is as much a detriment to writers as a boon. I remember W. Somerset Maugham thought this about the manual typewriter. Where did he write about this? In *The Summing Up*, perhaps, that never-bettered book of sage counsel from an accomplished writer based on his own long, successful career.[*] I have always believed that every would-be writer could learn more from this volume than from attendance at any number of writers' workshops, seminars, courses, lectures, readings, and all the other conveyers of advice and so-called instruction that profitable commerce offers the eager but unwary student of the writer's craft.

Oh well. In order to locate the book, I have to leave the computer before I have entered a single word of the work in progress, this sickly and unformed work. I find it necessary to go out of the study to find the book. There it is, in its elegant black cloth binding and gold stamping. I sit on the couch in the library to scan its more than three hundred pages for the quotation I remember imperfectly. But I don't find what I'm looking for.

[*] Published in 1938 in London by William Heinemann. It is well named, written after Maugham had published twenty-one novels and twenty-five plays.

I put the book aside. Once seduced, I know perfectly well I'll come back to it, so I leave it at another of my reading stations (beside the couch on which I sometimes nap). I decide to look for it in last year's notebook that, I now dimly think, might contain those good words.

It takes a little time to *find* the notebook, but I do. And then more time to find the quotation. Rejecting the temptation to read other, perhaps-useful quotations and aphorisms I had put down here for future reference, I am pleased finally to come upon the one I want:

> I think I must be the last professional writer to write everything he has written with his own hand. All authors now use a typewriter. I wish some learned professor of English would think it worth his while to write a brief treatise on the possible difference this may make in the production of literature now that every author uses a machine on which to express himself. Will he write more succinctly or, contrariwise, will the facility which the practiced typist acquires induce him to write more verbosely?

I have no date for these words, or even a location for them in Maugham's voluminous works. But they must belong to the time of the manual typewriter which is now ancient history, with the passing of the short era of the electric typewriter, and with the arrival of the age of the word processor.

I believe that the computer, with its adjuncts of software spellers and thesauruses, is now a serious enemy of literature, worse than bottom-line publishers and million-dollar advances. If the manual typewriter seemed to threaten to change the nature of prose in Maugham's time, think what the computer may do in ours: create long and then longer books. For torrents of words seem to spring easily from fingers to keys to fine-looking display to printout. As a result, the age of the very fat book is now upon us. Someone told me a good word for it: *bibliobesity*.

Another danger: The computer may produce many books with identical vocabularies. How many writers in the future will select words from the same program's limited thesaurus? However, one thing is quite certain. What the computer user *does* produce will be correctly spelled.

Why do I indulge in this long digression? It happens every time I sit down to the computer and consider the efficacy of the damnable instrument. Rarely am I able to do any original writing on it; I have not been able to teach myself to do this. I don't know how to commit my first ideas and sentences to the prolixity-tempting machinery. But for second drafts, printouts and rewriting, and then printing out again, rewriting and returning to the printer: it is fine for those things. It saves the cost of a typist who may have to do copies of three or four drafts at a dollar and a half or more a page.

During the winter, my friend Bill Henderson, founder of the Lead Pencil Club and a noted publisher, urged me to watch *48 Hours,* a TV program that had interviewed him about his club, which is opposed to all modern writing technology developed after the #2 lead pencil. I do not watch television but that night, to see him, I did, only to be stunned by the jumpy, sight-jiggling, sound-offending, chopped-into-ten-second-takes show. Only a few segments were of any length to be intelligible. The novelist Gay Talese upheld the use of the typewriter by the writer, but not by a typist or copyist. He said that as he typed each successive draft of a novel he corrected, changed, and revised, so that the typing process itself produced a useful, more improved version.

The entire hour turned out to be a celebration of the progress that technology had provided for communication. My friend was given about fifty seconds on the tube. Then he disappeared, not to be heard from again.

With Talese and his typewriter in mind, I think about the computer and the instant corrections I make on an already correct-looking piece of writing. It has not the same curative effect. Perhaps this is why I cling to starting from what can quite literally in my case be called scratch. Those handwritten pages now clipped to the board *look* unfinished, *are*, indeed, unfinished, and probably will not be finished for some time to come.

Having spent valuable morning time thinking about the machinery of writing and the advantages of manual methods over mechanical ones, I am finally getting down to the work itself. I start. I consider a new project at hand, a curi-

ous melange of history and fiction, a genre ("faction," I
think Truman Capote called it) I have contributed to in a
minor way ever since 1979 when I wrote a mostly fictional
novel about real persons.

There are times when I think such work displays a singular lack of imagination or, at least, an acknowledgment
that the characters have not come forth fully formed (as
did Athena, in armor, from the brow of Zeus) from my
imagination with no debt to real persons. I am told by critics that this is a sign of the absence of the capacity to in-
vent.

Yet I cling to the idea that there is something fascinating about tinkering with facts well known to the
reader. In this way I have borrowed from the known biographies of the Edward MacDowells, Marilyn Monroe,
Greta Garbo, John Gilbert, Gertrude Ederle, Diane Ar-
bus, Sylvia Plath, and other public figures. The armature,
their actual lives and the vision the public holds of them,
is often my given. What I tried to do in the fiction that uses
them is to imagine a fully fleshed-out body from the skele-
ton of facts, decorating it with possibilities, variations, and
angles, as a photographer's proof sheet provides many
slightly variant views of a single face.

Before I move the description of a building on a street in
New York in 1917 (the Beaux Arts studios on the corner of
Sixth Avenue and Fortieth Street) from clipboard to
screen, I consider, as I do every day in the long silent inter-

stice between turning the power on and committing my fingers to the keyboard, the persona of my heroine. She is a painter,[*] hardly known to the public and barely recognized in her day (she died during World War II). She led a curious, untraditional private life with her revered mother and two sisters, and an intriguing social life among the artistic figures of her day. The members of her circle were Marcel Duchamp, Virgil Thomson, Carl van Vechten, Alfred Stieglitz, Leo Stein, and many others.

I mull over the problem of narrator. I have assigned the painter to this task, but every day I become more aware of what a limitation this is. How much insight is she capable of? How much can she know of the inner lives of the artists and writers who come to her salon, of the fascinating matriarch of her family, of her two strange sisters? I wonder if I should start over, assigning the telling of the story to the sister who survived her (and, I believe, was left her diaries) or to the friend who curated her posthumous show at the Museum of Modern Art or, for that matter and the simplest solution, to me? Who can best tell this story of failure, talent, and feminine retirement from the male world that I have guessed at and embellished? I cannot decide. In exasperation, I inadvertently knock the pages from the clipboard. As I bend to retrieve them, I see a little

[*] A sad addendum to this literary intention: Before this book went to press, *two* exhibits of Florine Stettheimer's work were held in New York, thus stymying my plan to fictionalize this "neglected" painter. All this happening after total neglect and fifty years since her last exhibit!

rectangle of paper I have pasted to the board. It was printed more than fifteen years ago for an elderly patron of our store in Washington. He died a few years ago, leaving instructions that Wayward Books was to be offered his library and papers, among which was this slip of paper. Intended as a credo for someone working at a handpress, as our friend did for much of his life, I use it for my daily life and apply it to activity at the computer. It reads:

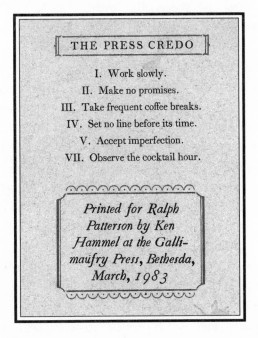

THE PRESS CREDO

I. Work slowly.
II. Make no promises.
III. Take frequent coffee breaks.
IV. Set no line before its time.
V. Accept imperfection.
VII. Observe the cocktail hour.

Printed for Ralph Patterson by Ken Hammel at the Gallimaufry Press, Bethesda, March, 1983

As I always do when I reach III, I stand, intending to obey that injunction. I need coffee, I think, although on this day I acknowledge I have accomplished nothing to deserve it. And, as is my custom before I leave the little credo, I try to decide what instruction VI might have been. It is missing here, and I have wasted hours trying to write a line for it. I wonder if it might have been: Make changes without rancor or resentment. Or: Take a nap after lunch. Or: You have done enough for this day. Or: Ignore whatever you have done thus far. Or (suitable for this day): Do not dwell on being trashed. No matter. I depart for the kitchen to take a coffee break.

I make the passage from study to kitchen, from computer to stove, a path taken so often that now I look for signs that the carpet is beginning to wear. Suddenly I remember, as I pass a bookcase and touch a book to even it up on the shelf with its companions, that there was a volume my bookseller companion urged me to look at if I am thinking of writing about an ordinary day in my life.

She said she remembered reading it when she was a young student in Paris at the Sorbonne. She found that it had recently been translated and was in print, so I had ordered *The Voyage Around My Room** by Xavier de Maistre from Nick's bookstore in Blue Hill. Last week I drove the twenty-two miles to retrieve it, sat down and read it at once. Now I think about it, as I perform the same kind of acts that de Maistre did in his book.

He was an eighteenth-century aristocrat with the title of count, who became an army officer, won a duel with

---

* Translated by Stephen Sartarelli and published by New Directions in 1994.

another officer, and was punished by being put under house arrest for forty-two days. To amuse himself, or better, "to beguile his solitude," as Richard Howard described the experience in his introduction, he wrote *Voyage autour de ma chambre.*

Much of it I found frivolous and immaterial, from the viewpoint of use to my present work. But I enjoyed his first observations. He tells the reader that his decision to embark upon a trip around his room had the virtue of costing him nothing, unlike almost every other journey he might have taken. He urges the trip upon those who are sick or bored, the fainthearted, the indolent, the lazy, and all those who might wish to escape from "the pettiness and treachery of your fellow men."

The count proceeds on his journey, stopping at various objects of interest to detail their virtues. "Heading north from my armchair, we discover my bed . . ." and then on to other objects, pictures, the armchair itself. He describes what he wears on the journey (his "traveling coat"). His narrative extends to journeys outside the room and the house—presumably he is freed from his arrest—and then to discussions of his affairs with women and other exterior activities such as stargazing, none of this as intriguing as the confined trip.

The count lost me as a fellow traveler, but strengthened my decision to make a book of a day. If he had adhered to an extended and fully detailed excursion around one chamber, the minimalist in me would have celebrated.

Still, the idea of the tour makes me aware this morning, as I push back the book on the shelf, that I am moving in the same way through my room, dwelling carefully on every object I pass.

In my youth it used to be said that travel was "broadening." As I brew a cup of coffee, I think about this truism and decide that, to the contrary, now it is narrowing for me. When I travel, my attention is so focused on the inconveniences and travails of going abroad or traversing this continent, of seeing what I have been told I ought to see, of escaping from the hordes of fellow tourists armed with clichés and cameras, that the "broadening" experience never occurs. De Maistre warns his readers that if you travel widely "you are losing time for pleasure, while gaining none for wisdom." I think even the pleasures are questionable. If I limit my expeditions to one interesting room or, at the most extensive, to one day in one place, I will look not widely but deeply into the traveler rather than the trip.

I sometimes joke with persons who wish me to make journeys to large cities for the purpose of what is called book promotion. I tell them that I travel widely in Sargentville, the village of about seventy-five permanent residents in which I live. Today, even that trip seems a bit far. But then I remember that, if Count de Maistre disliked horizontal travel as I do, he was a very early traveler *vertically*. In 1784, the year after the Mongolfier brothers invented the hot-air balloon, he went up in it with a friend, and then wrote an amusing account of his ascent, which he called an aerostatic experiment.

While I have coffee at the kitchen table I read the local paper. There is an account of a woman in Ellsworth with OCD, which I now learn means Obsessive-Compulsive Disorder. She is forced by her OCD to clean her house continuously. No one visits her family because her husband and three sons are not allowed to bring people home for fear they will track dirt into the house. They must leave their shoes at the door and wash their hands several times when they arrive home.

She also has an affliction called trichotillomania, the obsessive need to pull out her hair, strand by strand. The poor creature is filled with dread—dread that she has not turned off the stove or locked the door when she leaves her house. So she returns time and time again to check "until her brain agrees with her eyes that all is as she thought it was." She believes that if the constantly repeated rituals of her life are not performed endlessly, something terrible will happen to her or her family. The French call her illness "the doubting disease."

Engrossed in the story, I think about the woman who lived with her family on the street behind us in Des Moines when my children were very young. Five or six times a day she would race out of her back door to the clothesline with a basket of wash, and an empty basket in her other hand. With a week's accumulation of dirty clothes lying beside the washer in my kitchen, I would watch with fascination as she took down two lines of clothes and put up the newly washed ones. Whatever the weather she performed this ritual: one day she hung out and took in five washes in pouring rain.

A neighbor who had gone to her door with some misdirected mail told me that the floors of the house were bare except for long strips of brown wrapping paper that ran from the door through the center of the hall and (he assumed) into all the adjoining rooms. The story was that her husband and children were trained to walk only on the paper. The house smelled heavily of Lysol because, another neighbor told me, she used the noxious stuff to scrub down the closets in the house every day, every closet. Otherwise, she believed, they would be instantly invaded by mold.

I once used the fear of creeping mold in a novel, and now this newspaper report of another obsessed woman tempts me again. My real fear, however, is that I will repeat myself in my fiction. Twice have I had characters, women of the thirties, read the novels of Warwick Deeping, their favorite writer. Should I assign trichotillomania to the mother of my three sisters? Or, because I liked it and used it once before, should I assign to one of the sisters an obsession with cleanliness? The old tend toward repetition: it may be a characteristic weakness of an aging writer.

There are other items of note in the local paper. I read that I can now buy postage stamps that are premoistened. If more reductions of human effort are in store for us, will there be anything left for us to *do*, any effort we will need to make that will save us from indolence, not even the exercise of the muscles of the tongue? And when we are saved from doing anything except pushing the buttons that turn on the television and the computer, *then* what will we do with ourselves? When the computer is programmed to spell, choose words, indeed, *think*, and all printed books have disappeared into CD-ROM, microfilm, microfiche, and audio and video tapes, then what? We will have infinite leisure but nothing to fill it with.

I sit still in the kitchen, absorbed in a reverie about the unthinkable future, ignoring the present. I resolve to continue purchasing stamps that require licking and to resist with all my strength any effort to drag me into the brave new world of endless technology.

Meanwhile, I look out of the window and see that our resident and omnipresent gray squirrel is now hanging upside down on the thistle feeder, his avid little mouth pressed against one of the tiny slits intended only for the nutrition of finches. I open the door and shout angrily at him. He jumps off, races away, stops, and turns to look at me. I know he will wait until I am safely back indoors to resume his assault on the feeder.

Doris Grumbach

On the short journey (around my house? No) from kitchen to study I take the path that goes through the library/infirmary. This big room has given our life a new aspect. It is an anomaly among our rooms, the only one in the house without a view of the cove (except of course for the downstairs bathroom which is viewless unless you leave the door open wide as you sit on the toilet and then you can see a sliver of the water).

But the bay window of the new room has a generous view of maples and other trees, giving me the illusion that I am living in the woods.

Here and there the bookshelves on three sides have small empty spaces, so I believe that I can still acquire more novels (all the books in this room are fiction, except for the floor-level, oversized art books) without having my old need to double shelve. There is a shorter, more direct path through this room to my study, but today I am full of dilatory tactics, so I walk the long way, passing the shelf that holds a small wooden replica of the old Metropolitan Opera House. I regard it longingly. It reminds me of a book I examined last week in the bookstore about the history of that lovely building: *Requiem for a Yellow-Brick Brewery*.[*] From it I discovered that the opera house had

[*] By John Briggs, published by Little, Brown in 1969. When the beloved old building was demolished, this turned out to be a nice book to own, a stimulus to nostalgia.

once been thought to resemble a plebeian beer plant. It never seemed so to me.

Every time I pass the reproduction I see the great hall in which I first heard opera in 1935. Margaret Schlauch, my literature professor, and I bought four tickets (each) for *Der Ring des Nibelungen*. They were for seats in what was called the family circle. I never saw a family up there, only indigent students and ecstatic couples and single persons absorbed in reading scores at the desks provided for such perusals.

Maggie was very well informed about the precise location of seats, having attended the *Ring* many times in this house. The fifth circle, at the very top of the vast theater, wrapped around it from one side of the proscenium to the other. We bought seats on the extreme left for *Das Rheingold*, on the right for *Die Walküre*, back again to the left for *Siegfried* and thence to the right for *Götterdämmerung*. In this way, by quarters, we accumulated a view of the entire stage, not for each scene of course, but, eventually, for a whole opera.

No music has ever sounded as grand to me as Wagner did in that wonderful building. Much of the time we stood for our quarter-of-the-stage glimpses, and then rested, sitting with our eyes shut for long periods. I do not deny that the new opera house in Lincoln Center is elegant and modern. In the sixties, when Maggie came back from Poland for a professorial visit, we went to hear (and at last to *see) Siegfried*. We sat in the orchestra. During the intermission we walked about so I could show her the beautiful, lush appointments of the new building. But still, we confessed to each other, we missed the old place, with its shabby seats, too steep aisles, peeling walls, and the glorious voices of Melchior and Flagstad coming upon us from every side, left or right. We remembered fondly the few times we were even lucky enough to catch a glimpse of those robust figures on stage.

One last stop. I find on the library table an opened book, *The Road from Coorain* by Jill Ker Conway. Yesterday I left it in that inviting position because I intended to come back to it after dinner, and never did. Now I pick it up and renew my acquaintance with its cool, impeccable prose and the writer's hard but most interesting childhood in New South Wales. I am tempted to sit on the couch in order to read more. Two paragraphs further on, I am still reading. "No," I say aloud sternly. Move on.

Seated at my desk, still avoiding a confrontation with the computer, I try to conjure up my projected fictional family of mother and sisters. They come before my eyes, I see them clearly, but they resist my pen. Voltaire said that "to hold a pen is to be at war." I should be able to make this transference from interior vision to pen, but no, my pen is too much at peace.

Colette wrote, "Only describe what you have seen and look hard at the things that please you, even longer and harder at what causes you pain."+ Oliver Sachs said, "It is insufficient to see; one must look as well."++ This morning I look hard at what I think I see, but nothing comes to the page from these specters. I sit, now entirely at the mercy of idle thoughts, and then realize that what has filled the empty spaces of the new work is worry about the newly published one in the hands of other reviewers, awaiting the slings and arrows of their judgment.

In my present state I look up two very early comments. *Publishers Weekly* thought the book's prose was "laconic" but was fair in the rest of its comments. *Kirkus Reviews* said good things about it and thought the prose and tone were "immaculate." I consider these contradictory views, which go out to the book trade three months before publication date, and comfort myself with Oscar Wilde's aphorism: "When critics disagree, the artist is in accord with himself."+++

Nothing depresses me more, no matter how consoled I may be by Wilde's assurance that *I*, not the critics, am right, than the memory of a bad comment on a book while I am trying to write a new one. Suddenly the whole enterprise, my career, even life itself come under hard scrutiny. "Why do I spend my time writing poorly?" I ask

+, ++, +++ I have no idea where these pieces of wisdom come from. I found them recently in a notebook of mine.

myself. "What use is all this verbiage to the state of the world at large, to *anybody's* state of mind?"

As a partner in a store for used and out-of-print books for almost twenty years, I have seen the sad, endless flow of forgotten books sold to us for very little, and then consigned to our shelves or to the storeroom for a long stay. Some of these were once best-sellers for which no one has asked in many years, or books that were published with high hopes, sat for a few months at most on the shelves of a new bookstore, were returned to the publishers, remaindered, and then fell without a sound into the black pit of totally forgotten work.

What other human effort, in the long run, comes to so little? *Oh Lord*, I think, and decide I will have lunch.

Sitting beside my sandwich and coffee cup are the galleys of Helen Nearing's book of aphorisms. While I eat I scan them again, hoping to find a single realistic, negative view of the virtues of growing old.

I find none. To her old age is all cheerful acceptance, sunshine, and pleasure, never the miseries of bodily decay, loss of faculties, slowing down of neurons to the brain, and responses from it.

My irritation at her one-sided view of the process I see so differently has now escalated. I stand up, spilling the dregs of my coffee, march into my study and compose by hand in my shaky (another curse of being old) writing, a reply to her publisher. I round up as many aphorisms for the other side as I can find, and add them to the letter of protest, to wit:

> *Few envy the consideration enjoyed by the oldest inhabitant.*
> —EMERSON, *Society and Solitude*

> *The older we grow, the greater become the ordeals.*
> —GOETHE, *Maxims and Reflections*

> *The fundamental difference between youth and age will always be that the former has in prospect life, the latter death.*
> —SCHOPENHAUER, *Parerga and Paralipomena*

> *I'm in my anecdotage.*
> —CLARE BOOTH LUCE, in *Town and Country*

> *There is no such thing as old age, there is only sorrow.*
> —EDITH WHARTON, *A Backward Glance*

I put the letter and the galleys back in their envelope, seal it, and leave it on the woodstove to be taken to the post office tomorrow.

I remember the day Helen Nearing came to the bookstore a year ago. She was close to ninety and accompanied by a young man, one of the many persons, I have heard, who surround her and sustain her old age. She wanted Sybil to stock one of her books. Sybil explained that she never sold new books, not even her partner's. Then the young man asked if she had any esoteric books. Sybil had not heard of this genre before, and wondered if he meant pornographic. It turned out he was looking for the poetry of William Blake.

⁓

As I stamp my name and address on the envelope to Nearing's publisher, I notice that the folder this rubber stamp rests in reads, "Limited Lifetime Warranty."

⁓

Now indulging in two Fig Newtons which guarantee me on the wrapper that they are low-fat, I tackle the last large envelope of the day. It is a reprint sent me by Bart Schneider, the editor of a very good midwestern review of books called, wittily, *The Hungry Mind Review.*

At first I am confused. Why has he sent it, since it comes from the spring 1992 issue? Then I remember. A few weeks ago I was listening to a very good recording of Ravel's String Quartet in F Major when a vision of my first Victrola came to me. I once wrote a piece about that machine, but I could not recall where I had published it. I searched my files and could not find it. But I *did* remember that I wrote something about it for Bart Schneider. So I wrote to ask if *he* remembered, and if he had a copy of what I had written. Yes, apparently, he did.

Now I have it back, in the issue that contains pieces by other writers on the subject of music and childhood:

When I was growing up, to be middle class meant to have money. In New York City, on the Upper West Side, and in my family, money had very little to do with culture.

My mother and father were "comfortable," as my grand-mother put it. My mother had two fur coats—a caracal (lynx) and a beaver. My father had many silk ties from Sulka's, spent his evening time in bed reading the *Daily News* and the *Mirror*, and had his nails manicured every week. The polish he sported, as I recall, was very pale pink.

But our apartment had few books and no means for making or listening to music. I was fourteen and a sopho-more in high school before I heard any, even contempo-rary, music like blues or jazz. My father listened to *Amos 'n Andy* on the only radio we had. It sat beside my father's bed. My mother, a reader, preferred to sit in the living room, where the light was good, and bury herself in a novel from Womrath's lending library.

An aunt of mine, frowned upon by the family because she worked and because she had lived with my uncle be-fore their marriage, invited me and two boys my age from the Brooklyn Hebrew Orphanage (of which she was a di-rector) to go to a concert at Carnegie Hall. That Friday evening Alex, Lewis, and I formed a friendship, and I be-came a lover of classical music. I heard a Beethoven sym-phony (I cannot remember which), something by Mozart (also gone from my memory), and a piece by Ravel. I think it was "Bolero," else why would I think I remember it? Bruno Walter was the guest conductor.

I was forever changed. My love for the books I bor-rowed from the St. Agnes branch of the New York Public Library was now joined by my passion for classical music that, sixty years later, still possesses me. I write to music, listen to it in the late afternoon, hear it live whenever I can, and transport my collection of records, tapes, and CDs with me whenever I move to a new place. When I tire of books, I sell them; I have rarely sold a tape or CD.

After that memorable evening in 1931, I wanted to be able to hear music at home. At first my parents considered this an outlandish idea. But eventually they came around to buying me a console Victrola, in part because my mother discovered that this instrument came housed in a handsome mahogany box that matched the living room furniture. When the top was closed, which it always was when her guests came to play mah-jongg or bridge, it looked very much like an acceptable sideboard.

But records remained a problem. I stored the fragile 78s in the only available sleeves bound into ugly, thick, brown albums. I stacked them untidily on the floor at the sides of the Victrola. My mother disliked the shabby (as they quickly came to be) look of these albums. So she had shelves installed to hold them in an unlighted guest closet in the hall.

Now the albums were effectively buried in the dark shelves behind caracal and beaver coats, unlabeled on the spines so that I had to dig to hear.

Sixty years later I still have a few of those albums that hold scratched but beloved records like Rosa Ponselle singing "La Virgine" from *Forza del Destino* and Kirsten Flagstad and Laurenz Melchior singing the "Liebestod" from the last act of *Tristan und Isolde.* They symbolize the entry into my life, through the kindness of Aunt Evelyn Ferteber, almost by accident, and certainly against the firm, oblivious barrier erected by my parents, of an element of pleasure, beauty, and meaning, without which I would find life far less bearable. As I age I discover that I have less and less of a hungry mind and much more of a hungry ear.[*]

I am still thinking about the little section of my life that led me to write this piece when, hardly to the point, I remember an amusing exchange between two musicians. Andrew Lloyd Webber, the composer of very successful musical dramas and a very difficult man, it is said, asked Alan Jay Lerner, another composer of successful musical comedies, "Why do people take an instant dislike to me?" Lerner, without a moment's hesitation, replied, "Because it saves time."[**]

I start up the stairs for an afternoon nap when I hear Sybil come in from the bookstore for lunch. I think I will wait at the bottom of the steps to say hello to her, but instead I keep climbing, afraid that she will ask me how my work is

[*] This narrative was taken almost verbatim from the *Hungry Mind Review*, spring 1992.
[**] Someone told me this story. I cannot remember who it was. And someone else asserted it was attributed to two other persons.

going. I close the door to my bedroom, settle down in my bed under the quilt, and reach for the first book on the table's pile.

It is a small, thin book (I am partial to such volumes whether I am in bed or not; blockbusters of great girth tire both my hands and my patience) written by a typographical designer named John Ryder. He is a man after my own heart who believes that book design is an art whose end is both legibility and suitability. I read what he says about the letter *e*. Its eye should be open enough to be read without any effort on the part of readers. "Such careful attention to detail must be applied to every written and printed letter, and not only to the letter itself but also to how and where it appears on the page—in relation to adjacent letters, words, lines of letters, margins."

His first instruction to the designer is to know and understand the author's and the editor's view of the work. He is concerned that the look of the pages "reflects the author's intention." I read the rest of his seventy-seven pages thinking, as I close the handsome little volume, how wonderful it would be if every book received such scrupulous attention, if all designers believed that "you must present an author's work to the reader without fuss and with design techniques as invisible as possible."[*]

Of course, I am aware that with fifty thousand or more

[*] *The Case for Legibility*, The Moretus Press, 1979. For another, coincidental thought on the letter *e*, see p. 104.

books published every year in this country, such attention to most of them is probably impossible. Vainly perhaps, I go on hoping that serious work would receive such close attention, that the appearance of a book in its entirety would represent the spirit and tone of the work, that legibility would be prized above the ease that computer-assisted technology provides.

I lie still, thinking about my long connection with the world of fine printing and bookmaking. It was another fortunate accident. Many years ago the American Association of University Presses asked me to judge its annual book and jacket design contest. I was surprised at the invitation, having no qualifications for the task except, perhaps, my fondness for good design often expressed in a column I wrote for *The New Republic*. I was told not to worry. I was to serve not as an expert but as an "informed amateur."

So I went to New York and met with the two other (expert) judges at the AAUP offices. For two days (it seemed longer, as I remember it) we looked at submissions from university presses, selected what we liked and then debated, disagreed with, and insulted each other about the reasons for our choices. I found myself lagging behind publisher David Godine, watching what he chose, listening to what he said, and learning fast, on the job so to speak, from his judgments.

I remember his saying, as we looked at the production

costs for elaborate books: "It is as expensive to produce an ugly book as a beautiful one." Or perhaps it was the other way round, that it was as cheap to produce a beautiful book as an ugly one. Whatever. What I remember best was his two-day instruction to me, a novice who had begun to realize that there was a good deal more to recognizing good design than my intuitive and often hasty judgments.

Following that enlightening short course of study with Godine, I began to do some serious homework, reading everything I could find on the history of typography, the lives of famous typographers and bookmakers, and the guiding principles of handpress printing and publishing. A few years later, I encountered a wonderful woman, Sandra Kirshenbaum, at a Center for the Book gathering in the Library of Congress. She told me she edited a magazine called *Fine Print* and invited me to review for it.

I jumped at the chance, and began a nourishing relationship with that short-lived but most elegant and informative publication. I seemed to have been one of its "literary" critics, asked to review books for their content first and then their housing, books like Colette's *Cheri*, F. Scott Fitzgerald's *The Great Gatsby*, Samuel Beckett's *Company*, and James Joyce's *Ulysses*.

I taught myself to be aware of the suitability (in John Ryder's term) of the unity of the total design to the text at hand. I learned by seeing (not just looking), studying, and finding the correct technical terms in which to express my informed-amateur views. As a result, I acquired beautiful books for our collection of books on books and fine-press books, entering a new area of aesthetic awareness from which I never since have been able to escape.

I know how endangered is the species of finely made books, especially those that are handprinted on hand-made paper, and hand-bound. In the face of the possible disappearance of books of any kind because of revolution-ary technical "advances," as they are mistakenly called, this narrow corner of human endeavor will no doubt soon be taken over by some computer and an operator-robot. But no matter. I have had this long love affair with beauti-ful books of excellent content and collected a few of them. I can take one down, gently, from the shelf, hold it care-fully in my hands, read its good print, feel its fine paper and satisfying binding, and know that there is this unique pleasure still available to me.

At this point I fall asleep for twenty minutes and then wake, John Ryder's little book on my face. I am utterly without any desire to get up to do the work I have pushed off into the afternoon from the dismal waste of the morn-ing. To put off the moment of sitting up I reach for another book on the pile, and continue to read *Lake Country Por-traits*, about William Wordsworth's residence in Grasmere.

It seems the great poet never owned property in the lake country—he was always a tenant. A passionate walker, he composed much of his poetry while striding about that beautiful countryside. Even if it rained he walked and recited his poems aloud in the fields and lanes around Rydal Mount. The country folk were much amused by him. They reported that he was "turble fond o' study ont' roads, specially at night time, and with a girt [great] voice bumming away fit to flayte [frighten] aw the children to death a most."

His devoted sister Dorothy often accompanied him, and wrote down the products of the "girt voice" as they ambled back to Dove Cottage where she then wrote them down. I think how lovely it would be to be served in this way. A dalesman was recorded as having said of the poems thus lovingly put down for posterity, that they were "aw reet eneuf, but queer stuff, varra."

There is much more in this book* about the poet who began to publish his work when he was twenty-three. At thirty-seven he seems to have lost his creative powers. He must have suffered a terrible sense of frustration and impotence in the arid spell of forty-three years before he died.

Faithful Dorothy's life ended in a rather similar fashion. She was an invalid during her last twenty years and suffered from premature senility. But she left behind a few good poems and a wonderful journal that records the doings of her famed brother and his circle of friends.

* By H. A. L. Rice. Sadly, long out of print, but other good biographies of the famous brother and sister are now available.

Frightened out of my inaction by this account of long in-
capacity and lack of creative power, I get up, go downstairs, wash my face, and put on the kettle to make coffee.

I think about the sad Wordsworthian history. It must
have been very hard to accomplish one's great life work so
early, and then be able to do very little more. Sad for him,
no doubt, but ultimately of no matter to the world at large.
Two centuries later, we do not remember the details of the
production of Wordsworth's great poetry, or its precise
time in the life of the poet.

When I regret how little I wrote before I was in my late
fifties, how I might have improved this new book that the
Times reviewer found so terrible if I had had more practice
earlier, I remind myself that perhaps the balance is better
this way—the burden of work shouldered towards the end
of one's life—so that there is less room and time left for
creative disappointment, long regrets, unproductive silence. Well perhaps, but not today . . .

It is three o'clock. The sun is out with all its fierce afternoon strength, providing some interior illumination for
my day-long block. Go to work, old friend, it suggests, before I start to set.

My good intention is interrupted by the ringing of the
telephone. Usually at this hour I allow the machine to an-

swer for me. But now I am standing close to the receiver and besides, I know perfectly well, I have nothing better to do. It is Anne Chamberlin, an acquaintance who is back from her winter residence in Sarasota for a short visit. Business, she says. I invite her to tea but she cannot come ("Time is too short"), though she invites us to dinner with seven or eight others. I say at once, "I can't come, but surely Sybil would love to." We exchange expectations of seeing each other next summer. We hang up.

Then I am filled with guilt because I have refused Anne's invitation. But the thought of dining with eight persons chills me, as it always does. I do not do well at such parties, perhaps because my hearing is poor or because, when I provide against this failure, my hearing aids pick up every insignificant peripheral noise from as far away as the kitchen and leave me in a confusion of undifferentiated sounds. I sink into silence. To the others, I'm sure I seem a sullen, bored, nasty, self-involved woman, which, in part, I suppose I am.

But there is more. I think my determination to forgo large gatherings and dinner parties has often to do with the amiable but unstimulating quality of the talk. Most persons have a store of "social" conversation for such occasions: local gossip, friendly exchanges of the names of mutually shared places and persons, details of their family history, their children's locations and lives, and other trivia. At first I do not mind this. But as the evening wears

on and nothing of general interest arises, I find my mind wandering, usually back to the work I was immersed in before I left the house. It is the same retreat I practice during speeches, readings, some sermons, and many pieces of popular music that fail to interest me. People notice this withdrawal and must resent it. I regret it but do not know how to prevent it. *Mea culpa . . .*

Anne's voice has evoked a memory of her mother, Jennie Learned, at whose dying bedside I sat two years ago. It was in the local hospital; she lay comatose. She was in her ninety-ninth year and was surrounded by a devoted caretaker and friend (also a friend of ours—Bob McDonald)

and Anne, as well as a few of us who spelled these two constant companions when they needed to get away for a few hours.

There was nothing for us to do for Jennie except to take her hand and speak softly to her when she muttered something out of her deep unconsciousness. Anne was told that this was Jennie's penultimate sleep, that the mass of blood pushing down upon her brain stem had granted her the gift of insensibility. She showed no sign of feeling pain, but now and then she frowned, opened her eyes a slit, and then closed them and emitted a gentle snore. Sometimes she seemed on the verge of opening her eyes wide, but she did not, and I, a watcher, was grateful. It would have been cruel if she was able to witness her depleted state.

Remarkably, Jennie Learned was almost without wrinkles or spots. She had clearly taken very good care of herself and avoided the sun all her life. While I watched her youthful-old face a nurse opened the window. The hot, stale air of the hospital room was quickly displaced by fall coolness. With the change of air, the patient became more active and moved her hand and foot a little. Long an inhabitant of Maine, she may have felt more comfortable with this suggestion of the outdoors.

Through the open window, cooking odors came into the room—lunch was being prepared downstairs. I heard an electric saw being used outside, its loud, raw, unpleasant sound cutting the peace of the room. Could Jennie hear it, smell the food? Was she wondering what was left alive of her exterior self? I would never know, although my suspicion is that the dying may have an inner awareness of which they show no outer sign.

Anne and Bob returned, and talked about taking Jennie home "to die in her own bed," Anne said. At first I wondered about this decision, thinking of how much harder they would have to work to care for her. But then a nurse came into the room to bring the pro-forma lunch Jennie would never eat. The nurse lifted the sheet to inspect her body. Jennie had soiled the bed, her diaper having slipped to the side.

"Oh you naughty girl," said the nurse and proceeded to change the bed.

For some reason, this address infuriated me. It reduced a dignified dying old woman to a child in the nursery. "Naughty" is an adjective that belongs to childhood; it does not apply to the involuntary bodily act of this defenseless person.

Of course I said nothing, swallowing my indignation. We watchers talked softly among ourselves, even laughing a little about something irrelevant to the central figure of this drama. Did Jennie know we were there? It is possible she did and, like me, resented the words of the young nurse. Did she shudder inwardly at our laughter, knowing that she was shut off forever from all levity? How terrible must be the happy sounds of the living who will go on after the dying have descended into nothingness.

Jennie Learned, daughter of the eminent American

composer Ethelbert Nevin and herself a lifelong lover of music who took voice lessons from a local tenor when she was in her nineties, died in her own bed without regaining consciousness. Her daughter and her caretaker-friend Bob were near her. She was spared the presence of the condescending young nurse.

At her memorial service, people spoke of her having had "a peaceful death." I wonder. Who knows if, under the motionless exterior of the dying, a furious battle—a soundless protest against the abyss—is not being waged?

The phone call has led me into this long meander on Jennie Learned's life. I thought about her as I stood at the kitchen window, idly stacking and restacking the pile of books on the table. I pick one out, Christopher Morley's *John Mistletoe*,[*] a writer and a book I much admired in my college days. I wonder now why I never finished it, and decide it must be because I have lost my place. Walking slowly back to my study, I thumb through the first few chapters, stopping short when I come upon his prescription for good writing:

> The three chief qualities of style are Clearness, Force, and Ease . . . the rule of Clearness [I wonder as I read why he does not use "Clarity"?] is not to write so that the reader can understand, but so that he cannot possibly misunderstand.

[*] Written between 1928 and 1930 and published by Doubleday Doran in 1931.

And then, a few pages later [I am now seated in the armless chair confronting the computer, ready to go to work if I can just put down *John Mistletoe*] he speculates on the evils of memory:

> A sweet and dangerous opiate is memory; it is well that we are
> rarely addicted to it. Even the briefest indulgence confuses the
> sense of present reality.

Is this true? I wonder. My retreat just now into the dying days of Jennie Learned makes the present reality more vivid in some ways. The sharp recollection of her and the others who were there, and *Arcady*, the beautiful Tuscan house on the bay in which she died, does not confuse but instead fills and intensifies the emptiness of this afternoon, giving it the density and dimension of a diorama. My life now, as it nears its conclusion, is composed of such memories, brought to the surface of my mind by some unexpected stimulus in the present. Rather than a sedative it pricks the whole creative apparatus into action. What other resource has the elderly writer for such called-up richness? Surely not the profusion of immediate experience that the young have at their command.

Before I put Morley's book on the floor beside my desk (I am too lazy to walk back to the kitchen to restore it to its proper place in *that* pile), I come upon another paragraph in which Morley tells of receiving, as an aspiring young writer, the rejection of a piece he had sent to a magazine. The slip read: "The Editor of *The Atlantic* begs to be excused from the ungracious task of criticism."

Lovely. For some reason, it reminds me of a sentence I tried to use for one of the yearly, ungraded comments (in place of the more plebeian report cards) for a private-school student in high-school English. Unable to think of a way to deal with total nonaccomplishment and tired after a long evening of trying, I wrote on Charlotte B.'s form: "There is no substitute for natural intelligence."

In those years I taught in a girls' day school which, I was convinced, accepted a few students on the basis of their parents' high income. I was not surprised when the headmistress reprimanded me for what she termed my dangerous levity and struck out my comment. What I substituted for it, I cannot recall.

However, I do remember that the comment I considered so apt was not entirely lost—nothing is, ever, on a needy writer. Thirty-three years ago I wrote a novel based vaguely on that school.* A copy of it is across the room in a bookshelf. Delighted to have a reason to turn away from the bright-yellow printing on the screen, I locate it, open to the scene where the teachers are in the Common Room writing their final comments. One teacher remarks that the ideal comment is one that says, "Accomplishment: very little. Ability: none." The heroine of the story says, "I have the ideal comment but I've never had the nerve to

* A piece of juvenilia, *The Spoil of the Flowers*, Doubleday, 1962.

use it." Then the line, "There's no substitute . . ." follows. My character had less courage than I. But at least I tried. Neither of us was able to get away with it.

I work. I type from my scribbly handwritten text into the computer, changing almost every sentence as I proceed, read it up there on the screen (the angle is still awkward for me. I am accustomed to looking *down* to read), make more changes, finish a page that happens to be one scene, print it out, read it, make changes on the printout, call it up on the screen, make changes on almost every line, read it up there, make more changes. Then I decide to wait until tomorrow to print again.

By then I will have thought of more changes. It is inevitable that I will hate tomorrow what I have written today. Ring Lardner wondered, "How can you write if you can't cry?" Today I can leave this page in the memory of the machine. There'll be time enough to cry tomorrow.

For me, writing is slow work, a snail's pace, to express my usual rate of forward movement in a comfortable cliché. There is no way of hurrying the process. If I do, I write badly and erase it or crumple it up the next day. There are no rules for writing fiction that have ever served me well, no matter how well explained they are. I have a shelf of books on *The Forms of Fiction* (John Gardner and Lennis Dunlap), *The Craft of Fiction* (Percy Lubbock), the *Art of Fiction* (Henry James), *The Structure of the Novel* (Edwin Muir), *Aspects of the Novel* (E. M. Forster), *The Author's*

Craft (Arnold Bennett),[*] and a host of others by lesser practitioners. But I have never learned anything really useful from any of them. The writer in whom I seem to be interested today, W. Somerset Maugham, observed: "There are three rules for writing the novel. Unfortunately, no one knows what they are."

The garden is very dry. The sun has disappeared under typical late-afternoon low clouds, so now it is a good time, though not the ideal time of early morning, to water. We haven't had rain for almost three weeks. This is fine for tourists but terrible for tomatoes and astilbe. So I feel no guilt about indulging in the pleasure of shutting down the infernal machine, striking *F10* to evoke the menu, and then hitting *X* that enters me into *DOS* (a fine nonword, an anonymous acronym that represents to me a vast, incomprehensible area, but it's *there*), striking out the magic key letters *cd*, and then pressing the power button on the printer and the computer, turning off the overhead light and the light that swings out on long, grasshopper-like legs to illuminate the screen. I change eyeglasses and slip off the black wristband I wear against the soreness of my thumb. I am filled with vast relief by this series of healing, or at least ameliorating, acts. At the end I know I will be able to stand up.

[*] Notice that I have not provided publication data for these volumes. I hope the reader will trust my view that they all make good reading perhaps, but not particularly useful instruction.

The light goes behind the screen suggesting, mistakenly, that I have finished some serious work, when in truth
I have only done a little less than a page this day. I feel
fraudulent, as though I have just been released from the
hard labor that has produced an undersized baby. But
still, for the moment, I am finished.

Outside on the lawn the hose is in a great tangle. Knots,
impediments, introverted extensions, everything to stop
the flow of water. As I uncoil it, I think of a book upstairs
that is a now-forgotten masterpiece, *The Gardener's Year* by
Karel Čapek, the Czech playwright who entertained my
youth with a dour play, *R.U.R.*, about the horrors of technology, and who introduced the word "robot" into the
English language. Later today, when I can bring myself to
climb the stairs, I will find the humorous little volume and
insert the quotation here:

With a hydrant and hose, of course, one can water faster [in comparison with watering cans] and, so to speak, wholesale. In a relatively short time we have watered not only the beds but the lawn as well, the neighbour's family at their tea, the passers-by, the inside of the house, all the members of the family, and ourselves most of all.

. . . A hose also has a special predilection for developing a hole somewhere in the middle, where you expect it least; and then you are standing like a god of water in the midst of sparkling jets with a long snake coiled at your feet. . . . When you are wet to the skin you contentedly declare that the garden has had enough, and you go to get dry. In the meantime the garden said "Ouf," lapped up your water without a wink, and is as dry and thirsty as it was before.

Meanwhile, I think I can remember the perfect first sentence of Čapek's classic dissertation on the subject: "There are several different ways in which to lay out a little garden; the best way is to get a gardener."[*]

I finish watering the deck boxes of New Zealand impatiens and the newly planted astilbe, which are beginning to droop badly, as though discouraged by our long drought. I have managed to stay dry because my hoses do not spring a leak. It is as if they too realized that any excessive waste would contribute to the desperate absence of water.

[*] Originally published in Prague in 1929. My edition came from the University of Wisconsin Press in 1984 and was wittily illustrated by his brother Joseph Čapek.

The remainder of the afternoon stretches out before me, blessedly empty. There is nothing I have to do until about six tonight when Sybil will come back from having locked up the bookstore. She will go into the television room to watch the evening news and after that come out to where I am reading and suggest we can now have dinner. I will have spent my afternoon leisure on myself, blithely ignoring the inevitable fact of dinner. She will be hungry and will say so. I will not have thought about food, but when she has brought up the subject I will decide I am hungry too. Neither of us will make a move into the kitchen. So we will probably not have a meeting of minds on the subject of dinner until we agree, without debate, to go to the Morning Moon, the local eatery in nearby Brooklin, for a late supper. We will both feel relieved.

For now, I listen to the answering machine, take notes on the calls that have accumulated during the afternoon, and then settle into a comfortable chair in what is, somewhat affectedly, called the morning room (if we were Victorians we might term it the withdrawing room). I return the call of a friend who has left a cryptic message on the answering machine. She is full of sadness and informs me that a friend of *hers* has just died of a heart attack.

"Did your friend have any warning? Did she know her heart was bad?" I inquire.

"No. She had just had a checkup, about a week ago. Everything was fine."

I extend my sympathy. Callously, we go on to talk of other things. When we hang up, I think how ironic it is to die almost immediately after being given what my friend called "a clean bill of health."

Then, because the freedom from work seems to have made me light-headed, almost foolish, despite this sad news, I remember the story I once read in a collection of Maine jokes put together by Bill Sawyer.[*] It is about an old Mainer, I'll call him Jim, whose equally old friend Elroy was not looking well. Jim persuaded Elroy to visit the town doctor and accompanied him to the office. The doctor examined Elroy carefully and said he could find nothing wrong with him, gave him a bottle of tonic, and collected five dollars.

Elroy left the office, came out onto the porch where his friend was waiting, and fell down dead. Jim went in and reported to the doctor what had just happened. The doctor thought a moment. Then he said, "I'll be darned. But listen—on your way out would you mind turning him around so's he'll look like he was comin' in?"

Ashamed of my levity, I turn the chair to face away from the cove and decide to read a chapter in a book I bor-

[*] I could not find this collection so I have paraphrased the story, probably not for the better. I think it was Downeast Books in Camden that published it in paperback, perhaps in 1985.

rowed from the bookstore in the spring: *The Companion Guide to the West Highlands of Scotland.*✶

It is two years since we drove from St. Andrews to those high, beautiful, snow-covered hills. I think about them again. But as I open the book a yellowed newspaper clipping falls out. It shows no indication of the year it appeared or the name of the paper from which it came. Its headline: "Put His Wife in a Madhouse and Eloped." Enraptured, I read the two paragraphs.

Everything about this story is puzzling and intriguing. The book it fell from was published in 1963, but the clipping is clearly much older. Why did the previous owner of the book save it? Because St. Andrews reminded him/her of the villain of the story? Because the name McGregor was reminiscent of Scotland? And then there is a puzzle in the report itself. Why did Mrs. Andrews's sister not rescue her and the children from the asylum long before the elopement? How long has it been since children were put into asylums with their allegedly mad mothers?

What I admire most about this short newspaper "item" is the force of the few words in the last sentence. It is not only placed at the end for proper chronology; it is also there to allow the reader to conjure up the unexplored events that occurred afterward.

I fantasize: The happy lovers sit at a small, round table in a café on the Rive Gauche, drinking and contemplat-

✶ By W. H. Murray. Published in London by Collins (1968). An old guide but it served us well. Scotland, fortunately, does not change much.

> ## Put His Wife in a Madhouse and Eloped.
>
> MUSKEGON, Mich., Jan. 15.—Mrs. J. P. Andrews, who was fraudulently placed in a private insane asylum near Detroit by her husband, who then eloped with Miss McGregor, a wealthy young woman of Jacksonville, Ill., has been released on the demand of her sister.
>
> Mrs. Andrews is perfectly sane, but is prostrated with grief. She married Andrews here and he has squandered her large fortune, leaving her penniless in a madhouse with two small children, the youngest of which was born in the asylum. Andrews and Miss McGregor are living in Paris, France.

ing how they will spend the afternoon. Safe from prosecution and possible imprisonment in the United States, free of all the confining nastinesses of domesticity, marriage, and small children, Mr. Andrews is now making a lovely new life for himself. He has used up one available (to him) fortune, and he is about to make inroads on a second supply of money. Miss McGregor will, of course, pay for the stacked-up saucers (Pernod?). Then they will be on their way, arm in arm, to the gardens on the Île de la Cité that surround the great cathedral of Notre Dame. There they may rest awhile in the back of that vast building, enjoying the music and peace of the evening mass . . .

A detour from the book on Scotland. A side pleasure of travel to a new country is the planning of the trip and all the seductive reading one does in preparation for it, and then, much later, the good time one spends remembering the trip and conjuring up, in times of tranquility, its pleasures. But since I am of a naturally dyspeptic nature, it is not often the pleasures of travel but the pains that I recall most clearly. At this moment I sit back from the pages of the *Companion Guide* to remember my disappointment with the little island of Iona.

We had driven early one Sunday morning from a small, lovely country inn on Mull to Fionnphort and taken the ferry for the short ride to Iona. The ferry was crowded with tourists, so we had a lot of company on the half-mile walk from the landing to Iona Cathedral. All of us seemed in the same hurry to be in time for the service.

From a distance the cathedral is beautiful, very simple in its Norman design and made of thick, rough granite that seems to be pink from the windy road. It does not appear to be a soaring building but one that looks staunchly, solidly impressive, surrounded by meadows.

Shepherded into one end of the cruciform church, we were seated with the late arrivals from the boat, so far from the pulpit that I at least was able to hear only about half of the liturgy. But what I could hear struck me as unfortunate. Here we were in a very ancient place, a building originally erected in the sixth century, destroyed during the Reformation, raised to a cathedral in 1550 and partly rebuilt, and then completely restored in the twentieth. Yet we were being subjected to a curious, hybridized,

or better—mongrelized service that was neither Catholic nor Protestant but a little bit of both, mixed with something that sounded to me like ecumenical pap, or more like an olio of Rabindranath Tagore, Eugene Field, and a dash of beat poetry. A minister of undetermined religious origins talked about her life in the States. Many minutes were spent taking up the collection, during which the tourists dug deeply into their pockets for evidence of their piety and appreciation. I sat stolidly, determined to give evidence by my stinginess of my dislike of the pseudo-liturgy.

After the service Sybil and I refused to follow instructions to join a fellowship hour. Instead, we closely examined the restored areas which, like the Mayan ruins at Labán, clearly display new cement and reconstructed pillars. Of course, one cannot fault such attempts to "complete" or "finish" an ancient building, yet regret that, like the monastery to the side of the cathedral, it was not left with its original ruined parts unreconstructed.

We wandered through what remains of the thirteenth-century nunnery of St. Mary, called by the guidebook "the most beautiful ruin of the whole seaboard." It says, "The stone is mostly pink granite quarried from the cliffs of Ross, varied with black schist and creamy sandstone. The low walls, rising and falling between tall pointed gables, have become a natural rock garden."

We had the lovely, vestigial rooms to ourselves. Silent and elegant, no other tourists seemed interested in the place. "Just ruins," I heard a lady say to her friend as they walked hurriedly by. Nothing disturbed our absolute peace. I could feel the presence of lingering, ghostly sisters, who, like me, must have preferred the authentic remains to any attempt at cement restoration.

My taste for ruins, born and cultivated in the Yucatán, is now a fully developed passion. I have tried to understand why this is so. Surely there is nothing romantic in my feelings but instead, I think, they stem from the conviction that less is more, and suggestion is better than full, restored statement. In England, on our way to the Lakes, we were lucky enough to be entirely alone as we wandered the ruins of Bolton Abbey, only part of which has been restored to form the current parish church. But the beauti-

ful, oddly shaped tower on which building stopped in 1539, the angels on the roof that date back to the 1200s, the ancient altar resting on the original floor tiles where Augustinian priests worshipped in 1154: how close to history and continuity from the past these places are, how holy they seem to have remained without a modern hand having tampered with them.

Rose Macaulay, the English novelist, was gripped by the same passion.

> Our ruined abbeys and churches are, as a rule, only too well tidied up and cleared, losing in the process who can say how much of mystery and nostalgic awe. . . . But, when too much

ruined to be tidied up, still the foundations and fragments of
the great abbeys lie neglected in fields and commons. . . . The
ancient church in the woods . . . has fallen into dilapidated
sanctity, hallowed and haunted.[*]

Dilapidated sanctity—yes. I think about the remains of
the nunnery at Iona, Bolton Abbey, and the evocative
walls of the twelfth-century cathedral on the outskirts of
St. Andrews, and even the huge Lady Chapel of the Norman Ely Cathedral in which hundreds of small statues
stand there, beheaded (except for one!) during the Reformation. I travel by means of memory, no matter how de-
fective mine has become, through these places I have admired. I remember their mystery, their decayed sanctity. I
am filled with nostalgic awe.

Odd how this end of the day is full of rich visions, all of
them originating with the sheep on a nightgown. The
power of small, unexpected evocations, "the germ of suggestion," Henry James called it.

Thirsty and weary from all this travel, I decide to have a
cup of tea. Late afternoon always has the feeling of fatigue
and emptiness, as though there was nothing there, no content to fill the time. Recently, the Center for the Book in

[*] I can travel without moving from my chair through the great ruins of the
world in her *Pleasure of Ruins*, published in England by Thames & Hudson
in 1964.

Iowa City sent me the first issue of a little publication it intends to provide its members, describing the mission of the center and its accomplishments—I find a copy of it here at the kitchen table. I admire its title, *Counter*, and the explanation (among other meanings) of the term: "The white space within a piece of type, the center of the letter *e*, for instance." It occurs to me that it is a good image for this time of day, for the tired emptiness of an unaccomplished day.

This first issue of *Counter* contains an interview with Max Thomas, a professor at the University of Iowa who is interested in commonplace books. What actually are commonplace books? They seem to have originated in the sixteenth century, the Elizabethan equivalents of modern blank books, into which translators and scholars copied their thoughts, aphorisms, poems, quotations, and suchlike ephemera.

There were very few privately owned books in those days, so people were glad to be able to compose their own from materials that came to them from all sources. Now we have so many books that we are overwhelmed by their numbers and unequal to their demands upon us for attention or comment or shelf space. The eighteenth century had far fewer, yet even then Voltaire thought, "The multitude of books is making me ignorant."

Commonplace books are what I have been writing, I conclude, not memoirs, as I have called them. True, "memoirs" sounds more impressive, rings with a certain status, but "commonplace" is less pretentious, a more accurate description of what I put down and, I am now glad to know, has the authority of history behind it.

Still nursing the dregs of my tea, and sitting lazily in the old brown comfortable chair, I find myself looking out at the shining cove and thinking about May Sarton who told me on the telephone a few weeks ago, in her lost, weak voice, that she was dying. It is probably true, because even with her powerful will to live in order to go on writing, I cannot see how she can much longer survive her series of illnesses, each one of which takes its toll on her once-vigorous body. By the end of our conversation, her voice was stronger, she seemed to have forgotten about dying, and talked only of a trip she was taking to receive yet another honorary degree. "This makes fifteen," she said.

I remember that when I visited her last month she

seemed much diminished. But she gained strength as we talked of her memoir, which would be coming out in the fall, of her love letters to Juliette Huxley scheduled for publication next year, of her selected letters that an editor was preparing for publication soon, and of her three volumes of complete letters, most of them "to come out before my death," she said proudly. Her biography by Margot Peters was to be published posthumously, she told me, and then suggested she might have liked it to appear sooner—her hunger for publication was so strong that it had not been satisfied by the appearance of fifty-one books.

"But I don't expect anything I write to get much critical notice," she said bitterly. "My *Complete Poems* came out last year and not one important publication mentioned them."

I commiserated with her, but sympathy from me was unwelcome to her. "*You* can't know," she said. "You have friends all over the place who will review you well. From all those years you were an editor and reviewer. But I am outside the literary establishment where all the currying of favor with each other goes on. I am either reviewed badly—Karl Shapiro said years ago in *The New York Times* that I was a bad poet—or not at all."

Every poor review May ever received was engraved on the tablets of her memory; she often quoted them to me. So I had no reply to this. I have my share, of course, but I cannot remember them. I think I can predict what will happen next Sunday when she reads the review of my book. On Monday she will call to say how sorry she is. Secretly, I suspect, she will be pleased, her voice will sound strong because, as La Rochefoucauld reminded us, "We all have strength enough to bear the misfortunes of others." Or, as he said in another place, "In the misfortunes of our best friends, we often find something that is not displeasing."[*]

And still I sit here, daydreaming. I think of Isaac Wheeler, my grown-up grandson, because as a young boy he visited me when I was staying at May's house in York. He liked to water her flowers with a heavy hose almost too much for him to hold. I have a picture of him at work on her hedge, looking a little like Čapek's "god of water in the midst of sparkling jets." This reverie leads me into another, the humor in Isaac's letter of last year while he was working in Washington as an intern and, presumably, collecting memorable sayings for *his* commonplace book:

> ☞At a Senate committee hearing: "This whole bill is an exercise in fertility."
>
> ☞His favorite oxymoron: "The recording secretary was decidedly equivocal."

I think of him now with affection, having been fond of him since he was a small boy. I go back to that summer at

---

[*] A postscript, written when this book was close to publication: My prediction was quite accurate. When her biographer, Margot Peters, asked her how she felt about my bad review, she said, "I'm glad." Three weeks later she died, finally at peace with herself and the world. I miss her extraordinary presence, indeed *force*, in my world.

May's (he must have been about eight or so then) when I took him to the York pool to swim. His friend Bobby was diving and doing the crawl expertly at the far end of the pool while Isaac clung to a kickboard for dear life in shallow water. Undiplomatically, I spoke of Bobby's expertness in the water and said I hoped Isaac would soon learn to swim. "All in good time, Doris," he said, as if to comfort his impatient grandmother who loved swimming.

All in Good Time. A memoir title?

I wander into the library thinking I will listen, for about the fiftieth time, to Glenn Gould's recording of *The Gold-*

berg Variations. But perhaps because I have traveled in Scotland today, my eye falls upon a paperback copy of *Lanark* by the Scottish writer Alasdair Gray. I read it when I came home from that trip, having been introduced to Gray by a bookseller in Edinburgh. I learned Gray was as brilliant a novelist as Anthony Burgess claimed when he compared him to James Joyce. In the British Isles Gray is famous; here he is hardly known at all. It is a pity.

Lanark is Gray's first book, a funny, inventive picture of what Hell might be like today and partly, I gather, of Glasgow. It appeared in 1981 and was an immediate success, starting Gray on a most successful career. The story I like about this book, the first Scottish novel I've read since Sir Walter Scott's *Kenilworth*, concerns the first edition. The bookseller told us when we bought our copy that it was too bad it was not a first edition.

"Why?" I asked.

"Because in that edition Gray inserted a sheet of paper that read, 'This *erratum* slip has been inserted by mistake.'"

I think longingly of owning such a copy and then, for no real reason, remember the road signs we saw in some towns in Scotland, graphic depictions in silhouette of stooped-over persons leaning on canes, and under them the words *Watch out for the Elderly.*

When we got back to the States we went to a British

goods shop in Kittery to see if we could order such a sign for the road in front of our house. Later they told us they could not obtain one. So we shall go on, optimistically walking along our road at our own risk. My working definition of an optimist is still a person who has not lived very long.

The vision I have at the moment of being run over on the road beyond our house stirs other visions. Again I wonder about my fondness for ruins and, by extension, the way I like to study the remains of burned-out houses as we drive past them slowly, looking for artifacts of their residents and signs of the kind of life they might have left behind. I feel an affinity for falling-down barns, some of them leaning desperately toward the road as though asking for help, others collapsing helplessly in upon themselves, and all of them suggesting to me the last, despondent days of bovine or equine habitation.

Abandonment leaves few traces behind. But my mind always works hard over the traces, recreating what might have been there, the lives wiped out or moved away, the warm existence of a past lost forever in the cold, unpeopled collapse of the present. Ruined Bolton Abbey was, for me, such a place. And yet, could it be that some vestige of life still clings to these places if only one were able to spot them?

Such remains are like photographs, still and silent, and

usually reduced to bare black and white. Somehow they remind me of what Ken Burns said when he defended the composition of his documentary history of baseball entirely from stills. He called the still photograph "the DNA of the documentary, an empty vessel into which much can be poured." And Tim Page's statement (in the introduction to *Nam*, a book of his photographs, I believe) that he prefers still to moving pictures: "To me, human frailty is rarely portrayed with moving imagery—it remains the domain of the still photograph."

I keep recalling Rose Macaulay's words: "dilapidated sanctity, hallowed and haunted."

As it is for many writers, words arrive unbidden in my head. After "counter" occupied me earlier, it once again echoes in my thinking. Did Gerard Manley Hopkins mean "empty" or "opposite" in "Pied Beauty" when he praised God's gifts: "All things counter, original, spare, strange"; was "spare" not unlike "counter"?*

Once I am able to root *that* word out of my thinking, I recall hearing the phrase "clear cutting" spoken yesterday from an acquaintance who was angry about the disappearance of first-growth woods in Maine. When I asked him about the term, he explained that clear cutting was a method of leaving behind a thin line of trees along the

---

* To be found in any good anthology of English poetry. I used *The Oxford Book of English Verse* in the 1972 edition.

road to obscure deceptively the complete desecration behind. Another terrible form of emptiness, I suppose.
Counter deforestation, perhaps.

I put the recording of *Goldberg Variations* on the CD player
and sit on the stiff Victorian sofa at the far end of the library to listen. Here the stereo sound is best, so I sacrifice
comfort for fidelity. I listen, no longer aware of the room
or the stiffness of the sofa, although my mind wanders
once to remember that George Dillon called music "the
beautiful disturber of the air."

Every time I hear the last notes of this extraordinary
work I think of the act of rewriting. The aria, the first
statement of the theme, is followed by thirty variations
upon it. I am filled with awe every time I listen because
the Bach arias are so simple. Allegedly named for Bach's
pupil, harpsichordist Johann Gottlieb Goldberg (allegedly, because he was only fifteen at the time), the *Variations*
were Gould's first album, made in 1955. Then, years later,
he made a digitally recorded disc of the work, the one I
have. I am convinced it is the best recording on a disc for
a single instrument ever made.*

All the variations are interesting, although I am not
sure I understand their complications, or what "discover-
ies" Gould said he had made in those twenty-seven years.
I would have to hear the album to begin to comprehend

* Recorded by CBS Masterworks.

what these were. But the fascinating thing is that, at the conclusion, Bach scores the aria again. So it is with what I do. Often I rewrite, trying all sorts of variations on the original sentence, only to come back finally to settle permanently for the first one.

For me, music is both a *Ding an sich*, a thing in itself, to be indulged in absolutely with no accompanying literary thoughts, connections, suggestions ("This sounds like the sea" kind of thing), and, on rare occasions, the path to an idea, totally disconnected from the pure sound I am hearing. Once I read that the aborigines thought their history was retained in their memories as music, not in the spoken word. I become aware of the truth of this when something from the past rises out of a phrase of music.

As the Bach aria comes to a close, I consider going back to the computer in the next room. I wonder if I have enough of my day's original store of energy to write anything of worth at this late hour. But now that I have accomplished so little, another memoir—this daybook—has suddenly metamorphosed in my thoughts into a truly commonplace book, not worth doing.

I realize I am echoing Sybil's opinion about such books. Once, when I was halfway through a second memoir, she said that this enterprise rather repelled her. She could not understand parading one's self out there for everyone who reads the book to see. It is a kind of self-promotion, she thought, and somewhat ignoble. Philip Guedalla wrote much the same thing, that "autobiography is an unrivaled vehicle for telling the truth about other people," and only rarely about oneself.

I argue with Sybil that memoirs contain the barely visible tip of the iceberg of self, that most of "the truth" is not revealed in their pages. What is put down seems to the writer to have some commonality with those out there in the world, ideas and observations that do not come from self-revelation alone. And, since these ideas usually arrive when one is alone, indeed, has been alone for some time, I often trust their veracity.

Now that I am tired out by nonaccomplishment, I go on thinking of solitude. When I finished writing a book about it some years ago, I knew I still had much to learn. I have been acquiring that knowledge ever since, from books, in conversations with acquaintances, and in letters from well-informed correspondents. Most of all, I continue to be educated in that blessed state in those rare moments when I am alone.

Not long ago I was brought up short in church by the reading of the Forty-Sixth Psalm: "Be still, and know that I am God." After that sentence, or better, admonition, I heard little else. I thought about it for days afterward. It served as confirmation of what I have begun to sense, that it is not in activity, even charitable activity, or during communal recitations of prayers, or in the face of one's beloved, or even in the omnipresence of the beauty of the world outside one's windows, that one knows God, but in stillness.

Again, *staying put* intrudes upon this reverie—to stay put is very hard, since we tend to equate movement with being alive. And yet staying where one has been put, in stillness, is perhaps the most alive one can become.

Alfred North Whitehead, famed logician, mathematician, and philosopher, thought that "religion is solitude in community." I am not sure I understand this. For me, solitude in community cannot be attained. I find myself playing around with these three powerful nouns until I arrive at: Religion is community (with God) in solitude. Or even: Religion is staying put (with God) in solitude.

The phone ringing saves me from further introspection. It is someone wanting to know if I would lead a three-day workshop on fiction writing. I sigh, say "no" as politely as I am able, and hang up.

Back in my chair, watching the tide move out almost imperceptibly, I review for the nth time my feelings about the scams that disguise themselves often as writing workshops. Moved by my indignation, I go into my study to find the folder in which I have saved the two leaflets that came in the mail last summer.

The first, on bright yellow paper, is headed: "DOWN-EAST MAINE WRITER'S WORKSHOP." Underneath the blazing title it reads: "LEARN TO WRITE and HOW TO GET YOUR WRITING PUB-

LISHED!" and following that, "CALLING ALL WRITERS—NOVICE, INTERMEDIATE AND ADVANCED." The offering is for a two-day "sampler" and a five-day "intensive" session.

The florid prose informs me that the "sampler" is my opportunity to "taste-test" several "writing environments." These include fiction, nonfiction, writing for children, and newsletters. (For some reason, poetry is not included.) For $195, in two days, I am promised what the director-teacher calls (accurately, I am sure) a "quickie course," ending in "a super, optional New England seafood dinner." I am confused, trying to understand how the dinner that ends the course can, at the same time, be optional. But no matter. Perhaps the true reward for the "writing potpourri," as it is called elsewhere on the leaflet, is the "valuable certificate" of completion it offers.

The five-day "more thorough study of writing" will include half a day spent on marketing my writing, "including info on copyrights, agents, & electronic submissions." I notice with interest that the full five days are somewhat diminished by two free afternoons "to savor lovely area sights &/or fall activities," as though the concentrated stress of the other hours required these necessary breaks. At noon of the fifth day there will be served "a fun New England seafood luncheon." Optional.

This extended period of learning (for $395) will also conclude with the granting of the valuable certificate. But in addition I am promised my "personal notebook" (I notice that the writer of the leaflet uses tautology freely) which will be filled with professional "tips of the trade." (She also favors the free use of the cliché.)

In the folder is a second leaflet that arrived a month later. It is in response to my nonresponse to the first mailing, and is on salmon-colored paper. The offerings have been made more alluring. The short course now promises a mystery "special guest" who has been invited to the optional dinner, as well as my own personal notebook. Urgency is added: I am warned that class size is limited to 35, so I am entreated to "sign up TODAY!"

An interesting note of *amour-propre* is sounded: "Be

good to yourself for a change. Don't miss out. Register TODAY to assure yourself of a place!" Now I see I can take both courses for $550. For this "special rate" I will obtain "ALL THE FUNDAMENTALS you need to make writing your profession for life. This is your opportunity to immerse yourself in *the very best!*," an ambiguity not offered in the earlier mailing. A plaintive note of hitherto-deprived living is added: "Consider doing something for YOURself and your future for a change."

I am moved by a vision of the poor souls persuaded to attend the sessions who have in their past lives been deprived of opportunity and goodness until the moment they mail off their checks to the director and prepare for the trip, armed with the necessities listed: "a chair pad, a pocket thesaurus, enthusiasm, and a sense of humor. Also helpful would be a small portable typewriter or notebook computer and printer."

Fun is the emphasis of these workshops. To reassure me that there will be absolutely no diminution of joy, I am told there will be "No grammar! No punctuation! No drills! No dull or boring anything!" Clearly there will be No spelling! because spelling is not the director's strong point; twice in the first leaflet and three times in the second the word *accommodations* has been misspelled, an important word since it becomes clear that neither rooms nor meals are included in the special reduced fee. And note: if the leaflets are any representation, the exception to

"No punctuation!" will be the exclamation point which is sprinkled throughout the heated prose like birdseed on snow.

I am not to worry about the pricey fee, the director assures me, for "If you learn and perform your craft well [presumably in two or five days] you'll be paid 'real money.'" I will succeed as "hundreds" of her students have (none is named), and the director-teacher's qualifications are only inexactly sketched in. For twenty-five years she has been a successful author of books, newsletters, and magazine and newspaper articles, for twenty years a "staff editor for several national and international publications." I look in vain for the names of any of these.

I have been told by friends in various parts of the country that this kind of scam—I can think of no kinder word—is practiced widely. It has joined all the other instant opportunities offered the unwary and innocent for self-satisfaction, fame, and riches. Publication seems to carry a special enchantment. One will be famous and wealthy without daily and lifelong dedication to the craft, without unremitting industry, talent, or perhaps, luck. To promise an aspirant that two or five days, surrounded by thirty-four other people, will be enough to acquire "the tools of the trade," is deceitful, even criminal. The director could be prosecuted for fraud and for not printing, as an epigraph at the top of her yellow- and salmon-colored mailers, what Margaret Walker said about the craft: "A

writer needs certain conditions in which to work and create. She needs a piece of time; a peace of mind; a quiet
place; and a private life."[*]

Sitting alone in the morning room, waiting for Sybil to
come back from the bookstore, I think about what I said
recently to a writer's conference in Maine:

> Writing is a most solitary occupation. If you are bent on fol-
> lowing it, ignore all such gatherings as this, all workshops,
> seminars, classes, meetings, readings, sessions. Turn away
> from friends, family, society in particular, and the world in
> general. Only there, in the room with closed doors and the
> blinds drawn against the seductive outdoors, with the phone
> turned off, will anything good or useful come to you.
>
> Then you will have to return to that place, again and again
> and again, to rewrite what you thought you had got right yes-
> terday. Only by doing this for years will you learn how to
> write, alone and lonely.

I ended by telling the audience to go home right away,
and start. I should have added, "Buy a copy of Maugham's
The Summing Up, read it, and start again. And again."

Probably I went on too long with this message. I don't
remember. The patient audience stayed in their seats,
awaiting the next dispenser of advice, perhaps more to
their liking. "Few persons are saved after the first twenty
minutes of a sermon," Mark Twain once said.

[*] I found this in *The Writer on Her Work*, by Janet Steinberg (1980).

It is five. No sign of Sybil yet. It may mean that she has had a good day in the bookstore. So it is taking a little time to do her daysheet, her account of sales, tax receipts, expenses, and such matters which she keeps for every day the store is open. Hers is a financial commonplace book that usually displays profit, unlike mine of today, I think, which shows only loss, some loss of reputation, surely, after the disastrous *Times* review, much loss of time from not being able to write.

This is a good time of day, the approaching end of my solitude, and the dying of sunlight on the cove. I turn my chair to face it, thinking for some reason about grandchildren, mine and Sybil's. It is curious that I remember my children, now in their forties, and my grandson, twenty-four, most often when they were very young. *Anamnesis*, the Greek word for remembrance of the past, seems to have its strongest sticking point in childhood. Sybil has recently been presented with a very small grandson. I heard her tell her brother, Joel, about the happy event.

"How big?" he wanted to know.

"About six pounds and eighteen inches long."

"I caught a trout that size just last week," he said.

That story will probably linger long in her memory, like my recollection of my grandson's book which he wrote when he came to visit me at the age of eight, I think it was. I forget the title, but I know it had a title, printed carefully on the first page, and "By Isaac Wheeler" in somewhat larger letters underneath. There was a table of contents, with the numbers of many chapters listed, the contents and pages to be filled in later, a somewhat arcane (to me) but well-drawn frontispiece, and, following that, some blank pages. On the last page was the biography of the author:

> Isaac Wheeler is in third grade and wants to be a cartoonist when he grows up. This is his first book. His grandmother, Doris Grumbach, is also a writer.

I cannot remember too much about my own first book although it was published. But I recall every detail of Isaac Wheeler's.

Six o'clock. I hear a car door shut in the distance, footsteps on the gravel, and then the squeaking of the screen door. Sybil is back from the store where she sells used, out-of-print and medium-rare books, having made what she calls her hundred-yard "commute." She stretches out in the chair at the window across from me, expresses her tiredness after seven hours of buying books, selling books, cleaning and covering and pricing new arrivals. She tells me as she takes off her shoes that today she came upon a book on sailing the coast of Maine, entitled *Fifty Years of Fortitude.*[*] I decide if the author hears about my title he

[*] By Kendrick Price Daggett. It is about the maritime career of a nineteenth-century Kennebunk, Maine, sea captain, John Blaisdell, interestingly written by his great, great, great grandson.

will be sure I have cribbed it from him, when actually I used García Márquez's celebrated *One Hundred Years of Solitude* as the model for my book's name.

We decide to have a companionable glass of Merlot while she tells me about the goings-on at the store. While I pour wine and find some rather stale crackers in the cupboard, I remember the story she brought back from the bookstore yesterday. A customer reported she had gone into a new bookstore to buy a copy of *Fifty Days of Solitude* and was told they were out of it. "But," said the helpful clerk, "we *do* have a copy of García Márquez's novel. It's about one hundred years, so if you buy it you will get much more for your money."

Sybil's back is troubling her, from the weight of the books she has been moving out of her van today and into the storeroom of the store. I remind her of her fantasy-intention, conceived in England years ago, of dealing only in miniature books, a flourishing trade in London where there was an entire bookstore across from the British Museum that sold nothing but tiny, elegant books, about two to three inches square at their largest, and did a thriving business. Three small display cases would hold a whole shop of wares, she said. In her weariness she now thinks of the idea with pleasure, as do I, since it fits well into my plan for reducing life to a fraction of its previous size, a decimal, a bare and satisfying minimum. In other words, a miniature.

As we drink wine, she tells me about some strange questions she was asked during the day. Visitors to the area wanted to know: "Can you make a living doing this up here?" and "How do you come up with these prices?" While I refill my glass, she tells me, regretfully, the replies she wished she had made. To the first query she might have said, "Well, I make out, with the help of food stamps and other government supplements." And to the second (because she spends hours every day searching auction records and price guides in order to price her books fairly): "Oh, I don't know. I just make them up as I go along or pluck them out of the air." She imagines the importunate questioner, not recognizing the irony of this, saying to himself as he turns away, "Well, I thought so."

"I have two suggestions for titles of your memoir," Sybil informs me: *Just a Minute* and *Half a Sec.* I laugh politely and then silently reject them both.

"To be an adult is to be alone," said Edmond Rostand, the French playwright. Seated here at the window with my partner and companion, the yellowing dusk in the distance over Deer Isle, I realize this is not entirely true. In this early-evening moment, I think about his observation and decide I know better. To be an adult is to learn how to parcel out at the appropriate time a part of oneself, and to be able to accept a similar offering from another. Children are always solipsistic, and adolescents are Ptolemaic in their concept of themselves in relation to the world around them. In my love of solitude I recognize much of the child and the adolescent that remain in me. But still, there are adult moments when I need (want?) more—the presence of a kindred spirit who obliterates my aloneness and enriches my cheerless soul.

During the selfishness that characterizes most of the hours of my day, I often look forward to loving more fully, to less *amour-propre*, after six o'clock in the evening.

At six-thirty Sybil departs for the TV room to listen to Peter Jennings report the news. Thoughtfully she closes the door behind her so the noisy, disruptive commercials will not disturb me. I stay where I am, having no affection for news on television, for what I have heard called "talking heads," and for what an old acquaintance, Rod MacLeish, called "professional mouths."

I think about telephoning my daughter, Kate, the mother of two small daughters who are due to visit here in another month. Kate is an ultrasound radiologist who told me when she called last week about an elderly man she had been examining by ultrasound scanning for possible cancer of the prostate. To have this done, the patient must lie on his stomach, his rectum available to the physician.

During the process, the old man turned his head to Kate and asked, "Young lady, does your mother know what you do for a living?"

Before she could reply, her attending nurse, who has worked for Kate for some time, said:

"You should know what her *mother* does."

I like that. I dial Kate's number.

While Sybil is occupied with the quick takes that pass for news in the other room, I read yesterday's *Times*. There is a mention of Milton Petrie, the retailer and philanthropist who died last fall. When I last wrote about him, he was ill, using a wheelchair in which he attended the charitable functions to which he contributed so generously. Now, seeing his name, I think back to the time I sat at his table in the Berg Room during a New York Public Library "Literary Lions" dinner years ago. I learned more about him from his obituary after his death last November.

He was the son of Russian immigrants, born in Salt Lake City, where, according to the *Times* account, his father had a pawnshop. At that long-ago dinner, however, he told me that his father had been a policeman in Salt Lake City. (Which could have been true—he may have been both.) When the family moved to Indiana, he went to work for what he called the Hudson store while still a boy and stayed until he discovered that the company had a policy against hiring Jews. (This was *not* in his obituary.) In 1927 he left to open a small hosiery store ("with his winnings from a crap game," the obituary reported) on 42nd Street in New York City.

The store went bankrupt. He repaid his creditors in

full, and with the bank credit he earned for doing this he started a chain of women's clothing stores that flourished and enriched him. Most remarkable was what he did with his money. Persons in need in New York City received large sums of money from him, especially the families of policemen killed in the line of duty (in memory of his father? I don't know), those requiring expensive cancer treatment, and many whose sad plight he read about in the newspapers.

Literally hundreds of individuals and families were saved by him. So were institutions. He helped to rebuild the Central Park Zoo and fund the New York Public Library, which, he told me, was across the street from his store, so he went there to read every night in his youth. Now, he said, he thought of his contributions as "tuition" payment. He provided professorships at New York University, though he never even made it to high school. He gave a huge sum to the Metropolitan Museum of Art for a European sculpture garden. Numerous schools, colleges, and hospitals in this country and in Israel, five medical centers, and countless religious institutions received large gifts from this extraordinary man.

What I remember best about him, however, was the pride in his voice when he told me, "I'm retired, so every afternoon now I play bridge with *very* good players." Then, looking over at Jerzy Kosinski, his "lion" of the year before, he said, "I admire writers very much. I always wanted to be able to do that."

The onerous question of dinner arises between Sybil and me. It is now almost seven and, in our usual fashion, we have planned nothing. We consider all the possible solutions: go out to eat, forage in the cupboard and refrigerator, go to the Eggemoggin general store nearby for takeout chicken (for me) or pizza (for Sybil). Or skip the whole thing and lose a little weight. We decide the last alternative is not practical because we will be starving by nine o'clock and then will proceed to overeat (if indeed we can find anything in the house to overeat).

Finally we settle for a quick supper at the Morning Moon Cafe, an odd name for a place we never visit except for lunch or dinner. "Quick" means we intend to eat something simple—and cheap—but of course it never ends up this way. We will be interested only in the most expensive entree on the chalkboard and fatally tempted by the richest dessert, *mit Schlag*. The dinner will be neither quick nor cheap, but we will console ourselves with the lack of dishes to wash. On our drive to Brooklin, we are behind a car with a nice punning bumper sticker: *Metaphors Be with You.* I expand upon the thought that the time will come when bumper stickers may supersede books. Children will be taught to read by their parents while driving very close to the car ahead and demanding they tell them what they see. All philosophy, all economic theory, all political thought, will be reduced to these one-line statements stuck on the rears of cars. This will be a fine,

simplistic approach to culture and intellection that will
suit my love of the minimal.

Sybil starts to tell me of two other bumper stickers she
has seen recently. She remembers one, and then cannot recall the second. She is taken aback by this lapse of memory,
but she excuses it by recalling her favorite remark by her elderly mother, when she was reminded of something: "You
don't need to tell me about it. I *know* what I've forgotten."

While we make the trip to the restaurant I tell her *I* have
thought of some possible memoir titles: *See If I Care* and
(for the final one) *How Many Times Do I Have to Tell You?*

At the door of the Morning Moon we encounter Anne Chamberlin, with whom we join forces in the last available booth (of four) in the small restaurant. It is the ur-Maine place, with booths, a few tables, including two almost up against the tiny restroom, which is often closed if there is a drought. A ceiling fan revolves on warm days. Local poets write poems about the place and type them up to hang on the walls, and local painters display their art with the poetry. The menu for the day is chalked up on a few boards also hung on walls.

The Moon, as it is known locally, serves well-cooked down east food, although recently Adam, the young cook, has taken to emulating upscale big-city restaurants and branched out into charcoal-broiled dishes that successfully disguise the original flavor of the meat or fish with a uniformly burnt taste. A baked apple-bread pudding, very dry, has replaced the old rich and tasty bread pudding.

No matter. We study the blackboards, shoehorn ourselves into the narrow booths, order from the one waitress who serves the whole place—an acquaintance who knows our preferences—and begin to talk. We enlighten Anne, who spends most of the year in Sarasota, about the events of our winter, the work we are doing, the news of our mutual friends.

She has a fine story to tell: She returned to her cottage in Blue Hill from Florida, opened a cupboard, and discovered her life's work, copies of everything she has ever published during a long career in journalism, had been cut into neat circles by what must have been a most literate mouse.

She says it was an extraordinary sight, this orderly destruction, so methodical that she was able to lift the pieces out and begin the tedious process of pasting the pages back together. It will take a long time, she says, but she is determined to accomplish it. I remember my own trashing this morning so I suggest the possibility that the vandal-mouse might have been a *critic*. I tell her about my old computer, which, in its last year, refused to accept my instructions. I accepted its rejections and repetitions as acts of literary criticism, and bought a new computer. It turned out to be more admiring of my prose. I notice that I do not tell her about the review that came this morning.

We talk of other things. I begin to say something about my growing dislike of large gatherings and dinner parties. I hear myself saying, "I am inclined to avoid . . ." and stop, realizing too late that I have made an oxymoron. These apparently contradictory words, which Theodore Bernstein says have "the startling effect of a paradox," make for humor, on occasion.* He cites one example, "conspicuously absent" and (less humorous) a figure from the poetry of Elizabeth Barrett Browning: "thunders of white silence."

---

* In *The Careful Writer*, published by Atheneum in 1973. A good guide to English usage, witty and instructive. All the examples I have used here are from Bernstein's helpful book.

Of all the possible figures of speech I learned about when I studied rhetoric—metonymy ("the White House" for the administration), anticlimax ("a gentleman, a scholar, and a good judge of liquor"), dyphemism (sailors calling a navy destroyer a "tin can"), litotes (understatement, as in "not bad" for "good"), and the many others— I favor the oxymoron, possibly because of the derivation of the word itself, from the Greek word meaning "sharp-dull." It is good to have once known (vanishing now in my late years) a language that can accommodate *in one word* such a contradiction.

We talk about the lack of rain in recent weeks. Drought up here means an unproductive blueberry season and vegetable gardens that wither and fail. I tell them that I have read recently in the *Times* that scientists from the University of Florida at Gainesville have made a chemical analysis of the bed of Lake Chichancanab on the Yucatán Peninsula. They have concluded that the mysterious abandonment of the great Mayan cities was caused by two hundred years of terrible drought, the harshest such period in eight thousand years.

Neither of my dinner companions seems as interested in this report as I. And I know why. My fascination with the ruins of the Mayan lowlands stems in part from the failure of scholars to explain what I prefer to think of as an unsolvable mystery. Prolonged drought is one explanation. Interior political conflicts, intercity rivalries, and overpopulation are others. But still, as I stand at the bottom of a great pyramid in the gray light of late evening, I prefer to be suffused with the inscrutable rather than with fact.

While Sybil and Anne make plans for a final meeting before she goes back to Florida, I continue to think about drought. Two hundred years of it on *our* peninsula and this tenuous civilization might well disappear. Archaeologists will attribute our abandonment to it. Eventually they will realize that we had gone elsewhere or died away because what water we *had* was polluted, or that the air we breathed was filled with lethal gases, or our food was so loaded with chemical additives that we could not survive.

Centuries from now, explorers will come upon vestiges of the ruined Morning Moon Cafe, and decide this was not a great civilization architecturally. But it may have been a place where the first sign of deadly drought could be seen—on the bathroom door of the restaurant there now hangs this sign: "Not in Use Due to Water Shortage."

We part from Anne and start the drive home, along the Reach that now is beginning to harbor some sailboats. Two new houses are being built along the road on the water side, extravagantly large and clearly very expensive. We wonder how long it will be before these elaborate summer "cottages" will outnumber the modest homes and omnipresent trailers and mobile homes that house the old, native population. Perhaps our civilization will fall from an imbalance between rich and poor, the overfed and the hungry, those with three homes and those with none. A fierce civil revolt against privilege and possessions could erupt, more deadly than the simple drying up of reservoirs and wells.

"Did you notice that the three gray-haired couples in the other booths almost never talked to each other?" I ask Sybil as she drives across the short, narrow Benjamin River Bridge.

"I did. Why do you ask?"

"I was thinking about what Gloria Steinem once said: 'The surest way to be alone is to get married.'"

"Hm. I suppose. After all those years of marriage, they may be bored with each other."

"Do you know what Ambrose Bierce said about a bore?"

"No."

"He said a bore was a person who talks when you wish him to listen."

"So. Got any more quotations tonight?"

"Not at the moment," I say, watching the sun disappear over distant trees.

At home we settle into easy chairs to watch the light die and to read yesterday's newspaper. I have eaten too much supper—even a piece of the dry, much-maligned baked apple-bread pudding—and can feel the mass of food making its reluctant way through my lower digestive tract.

This spring I had a colonoscopy. As I lay on my side, an invasive examiner sent a probe the whole length of my colon. I was able to follow the action on a viewing screen. The other day Tom Disch, a friend whose excellent books on many subjects and in every genre seem to pour out of him year after year, wrote to me that he had such an examination. "It was the most entertaining film I have seen in two years," he said. I too had found it engrossing, but for me it took longer than I had expected. The doctor acknowledged this and reported that I had some extra areas to explore. To my delight he termed this excess a "redundant colon," not unlike ": : :," I suppose.

Ever since that examination, I occasionally amuse myself by trying to follow the remote progress of my victuals as though I were mentally peering into a fluoroscope. But tonight I take my mind from what is going on inside me by picking up a book by Julian Mazor and turning to a story I read for the first time in *The New Yorker* in the late sixties. Called "Washington," it is part of a volume, *Washington and Baltimore,*＊ by a now-forgotten writer—forgotten, but not by me. I remembered the story as impressive and now I see that it is one of the best race relations stories I have read. There are five other stories in the collection, all very good. Since the book appeared, almost thirty years ago, I have watched for fiction by Mazor. Nothing has appeared.

＊ Published by Knopf in 1968. It must have had good reviews because my copy, a second printing, is dated three months after publication.

Some years ago I read a piece in the Washington, D.C., *City Paper* by a fellow[*] who went looking for Julian Mazor. He was as puzzled as I about his complete disappearance. (Salinger similarly vanished from view but somehow managed to parlay his dropping out of the literary scene into instant publicity and enduring literary fame.)

The journalist found Mazor. He was now sixty years old, lived very near the District of Columbia in Alexandria, Virginia, had "investments" and "reserves," and went to an efficiency apartment every day above a movie theater in D.C. where he continued to write. Today, as I once again pick up his book, it is six years later. I assume he is still there, still not publishing what he has been working on, still avoiding any semblance of being a public person, profoundly disinterested in literary celebrity. "It's the work that matters . . . I just want to write. I just want to do my work," he told the interviewer.

Since that long-buried book, Mazor has not appeared in print. I am in awe of such patience, such long concern for the "work." In 1963, the year of Mazor's only book, John Updike, who wrote his first book when he was twenty-five, published a novel. To date, his publisher, Knopf, boasts in a recent catalogue, he has issued forty-two books with them. And how many with other publishers? I do not know. Joyce Carol Oates must have a somewhat similar record—and May Sarton, of course.

It strikes me that such prolific writers may have been

[*] Mark G. Judge, in the 12 March 1990 issue of the paper.

moved so often into print by having a great deal to say. Or it could be they have a deep *need* to appear constantly in print. Or, gifted with style and fluency, they are able to write about *anything* without hesitation. Or could it be that some writers need to publish constantly in order to assure themselves that they *are* writers?

Then we have Julian Mazor, sitting in his room above the Uptown Theater. He may be polishing the most memorable novel of the last fifty years, to be read everywhere in the next century long after all the rest of the eager-to-publish persons have disappeared from literary memory.

It is almost nine o'clock. I sit watching the dark take over the cove. Only a small light at the point manages to cut through and reach me. I am tired of reading. I am tired of not writing. I am even weary of thinking, which earlier in the day was an agreeable diversion.

"Do you know how Alexander Pope defined 'amusement?' " I ask Sybil who is about to depart for the TV room to watch *Northern Exposure*.

"No," she says, somewhat wearily. I think I may have overloaded her with quotations today, but I cannot resist one more.

" 'Amusement is the happiness of those who cannot think.' "

"Interesting," she says. "Is this apropos of my watching TV?"

"Oh, no. It has to do with my thoughtlessness at this time of night."

She says she will see me upstairs later and closes the door behind her to the TV room.

I think about going to bed. I think I am too tired to make it up the stairs. It is at this moment in the long day that my increasingly onerous age almost conquers my resolve. While the rituals of the morning are usually accomplished with some energy, the required night ceremonies seem almost insurmountable: ascending the stairs, undressing, struggling into a nightgown, visiting the bathroom, even getting into bed and deciding on a book I will inevitably be too tired to finish.

I delay. Beside my chair is the theater section of *The New York Times*. I read that Patti LuPone, the celebrated star of the musical *Sunset Boulevard* during its London run, has been "dumped" (the *Times*'s word, not mine) from her role for the New York production in favor of the actress Glenn Close. LuPone, born in Long Island, must have hoped to come home to New York in triumph, but it was not to be. She is badly hurt by the firing.

But then I read that Miss LuPone is planning to come to the New York stage in her own one-woman show. In it, she plans to sing the hit song from *Sunset Boulevard*, "I've Come Home at Last." The *Times* piece goes on: "She has found a way to make effective use of them [her wounds] by spinning her own Broadway legend: the jittery, vulnerable diva . . . who wears her insecurity on her sleeve."

I am struck by this. I see that I now plan to emulate the diva, and make "effective use" in these pages of my wounds from the critic of my book, airing them in order to heal them, ridding myself of pain by writing about them.

So I stay seated, hearing faint sounds of the sitcom from the other room, and sinking into a reverie that is a mixture of despair and gratitude. Gratitude for this house in this place where the dramas and pleasures of the day are enacted. Near my right hand and so needing little effort to reach is my copy of Somerset Maugham's *The Moon and Sixpence*, and I open to the place of the bookmark. Again, I read the passage in my emended version: "a place in which I mysteriously feel I belong . . . here at last I find rest."

The sentiment is still very meet and right. Gratitude, resembling Maugham's, drives my weary self upstairs and gets me through all the rituals of retirement. I say the usual prayers, the one of Lancelot Andrewes that contains the fine line, "Pour out your rich pity and save all your People, O Lord," and the lines Robert Louis Stevenson wrote when he was dying in Samoa, "Give us strength to encounter what is to come, that we may be brave in peril, constant in tribulation, temperate in wrath and in all changes of fortune and, down even to the gates of death, loyal and loving to one another."

As it always happens to me at this time of night, however, prayer does not effect closure. I am overwhelmed by the catastrophes of the day—the failure to write and oh, now it returns, by the review that clouded my day and now blackens my night. After living with it for twelve hours I have not yet been able to come to terms with it, to bury it in the fortunate pit often dug by a failing memory. I tell myself some of the harsh words will be featured prominently in my obituary, may well be the major items quoted in my death notice.

But then, I laugh. I have a sudden recall of something I read a while back about Florence Nightingale. She was once very ill and was expected to die. Her friend, the writer Harriet Martineau, was asked to write her obituary. Martineau did so, but the famous nurse recovered and lived fifty more years, thirty-four years after the writer of the obituary had died.

Somewhat cheered, I bury the thoughts of this day, my rich self-pity, and escape into the oblivion that brings blessed forgetfulness.